THE (COMPLETELY UNOFFICIAL)

TARTAN ARMY
SONGBOOK

NEW EDITION

Also by Ian Black

Who Wants to be a Glaswegian?
Two (More) Andy Gorams
Weegies v. Edinbuggers

THE (COMPLETELY UNOFFICIAL)

TARTAN ARMY SONGBOOK

NEW EDITION

IAN BLACK

BLACK & WHITE PUBLISHING

*For Leslie, who has never been to a game of football
in her life, but who still tolerates me.
Just.*

First published 2002
by Black & White Publishing Ltd

This edition 2003

ISBN 1 845020 00 6

Text copyright © Ian Black 2003

The right of Ian Black to be identified as
author of this work has been asserted by him
in accordance with the Copyright, Designs
and Patents Act 1988.

British Library Cataloguing in Publication Data:
A catalogue record for this book is available
from the British Library.

Every effort has been made to contact all copyright holders
of the material in this book. If you have any information
on any other copyright material contained herein,
please contact the publishers.

Printed and bound by Nørhaven Paperback A/S

PREFACE

BY THE CHIEF EXECUTIVE OF THE
SCOTTISH FOOTBALL ASSOCIATION

I've been a member of the Tartan Army as long as I can remember, well at least as far back as 1966 when I saw my first Scotland match at Hampden Park. Only at that time, we weren't called the Tartan Army. Yes, we wore tartan scarfs, waved flags and were loud in support of our national team, but we were not called the Tartan Army. Someone somewhere may be able to pinpoint the origin of the description but, if not created by Andy Cameron's 1978 World Cup song, it was certainly popularised by it. Given the repertoire of songs now available to the Tartan Army, it seems peculiarly appropriate that it all began with a song.

Today, the phenomenon that is the Tartan Army has no equal anywhere in the world. There may be more fanatical supporters – think of Turkey for example – but nowhere do we find a loose organisation of supporters that is bound together in quite the same way through cultural, social and behavioural norms. It is a misconception that we are all Scottish Nationalists. What we do share is a pride in our country, a love of football and a desire to offer the hand of friendship to people in all corners of the world. As perennial underdogs in international football competitions, we understand what it is like to experience failure, but that does not stop us dreaming of success. Do not believe newspaper reporters who say that the Tartan Army does not care about results. Defeat hurts but, after a while and fortified by good company and a good few beers, life does not seem so bad . . . and the songs return.

At the Scottish Football Association (SFA), I have been keen to recognise and work with the Tartan Army to bring them closer to the National team. We have, of course, a responsibility to all Scotland supporters, particularly those in the Scotland Travel Club. But the emergence of geographical groups such as WESTA, NOSTA, EASTA etc give us an opportunity to canvass views on issues of interest to supporters. Through this, we have worked hard to create the right conditions for a much better home ground atmosphere at Hampden. The Tartan Army is not just an overseas travel club. The Scotland team needs the support and energy created by the Tartan Army to help raise their game but we also want to make attendance at Hampden a real pleasure. Again, we have turned to song as we have tried to develop the half-time party experience with enhanced sound systems, and set aside a musical instruments section for the Tartan Army. I'm still waiting to hear the string quintet.

As for the songs themselves, some are topical and some enduring. 'We'll Support you Evermore' seems to have been around forever. However, I also remember singing 'We don't need Eusebio, 'cos we've got Colin Stein.' Seems a bit silly now. History can be told in song, nevertheless, and I always liked the song 'We could not Beat Iran'. This now has a number of verses. Another favourite of mine is 'It's Just Like Watching Brazil', not sung with gusto at many games, but memorably sung at the opening match of the World Cup in 1998. Least favourite – not 'Flower of

Scotland', but 'Doh-a-Deer'. This is not the sound of music to my ears.

So, enjoy this collection of Tartan Army songs. Until our supporters settle on another song as our national song, the Scottish FA will keep playing Flower of Scotland before matches. One day, however, I hope to be standing there before a match singing a song for which Scotland is known the world over – 'Auld Lang Syne'. The words are memorable and entirely in keeping with the sentiments of today's Tartan Army. It would fit the Scottish national team more neatly into overall efforts to increase recognition of our special country overseas. I suspect the debate on our official song will run and run, but it is the unofficial, spontaneous songs for which the Tartan Army is now rightly known. Keep them coming.

David Taylor
Scotland Travel Club Member No. 143

Author's note: David Taylor and I do not see eye to eye on the odd thing or two, but I asked him to write this preface, and despite our differences, he did, because he and I know that these differences are vastly outweighed by our mutual love for Scotland. He also wrote to me saying: '. . . you have your opinion, you are a respected journalist and you are perfectly entitled to express it. I actually quite like the anti-establishment thing – it's in my character – so keep it up and give us a hard time on issues that matter.'

Respect. And how can you not love an SFA Chief Executive who signs himself: 'Scotland Travel Club Member No. 143'?

Thanks

to everyone who wrote, e-mailed and poured songs, chants, obscenities and blasphemy down my phone. I've tried to mention everyone and if your name is missing it is probably because I don't like you. Or it might be in the text.

Alastair Nicholson, Ruary McGregor, Ally Maciver, Gordon Forsyth, Peter Speed, Gordon Johnstone, Will fae Swindon, Wullie Anderson, Martin Mitchell, Ian Learmonth, Davie Carson, Mike McColl
and dozens of fanzines, websites
and anonymous correspondents.

For this new edition there are more than several new sinners to add. Most of them are mentioned in the text, but these deserve special mention for actions above and beyond the call of the pub.

Crawford Graham, Micky Ross, Euan Kerr, Louise Smith, Scott Fairs, Patrick Martin Lynch, Tom Small

Completely Unofficial Disclaimer

The views, comments and opinions contained in this book are entirely those of the fans and supporters. In each case, the author has reproduced these as faithfully as possible and neither the author nor the publisher accepts any responsibility for their vicious sense of humour, appalling rudeness or ready wit. Just as well professional footballers are paid a fortune if they get this kind of treatment every week, but the bucks, the burdz and the booze must be a comfort.

INTRODUCTION

Have you ever felt like ripping off your knickers, donning your kilt, drinking sixteen pints and becoming the latest recruit to the concatenation of chaos that is the Tartan Army, but have been ashamed to because of your lack of musical and lyrical knowledge? Fear not! Help is at hand.

The songs and chants in this volume were collected and culled both from the virgin foot soldiers and from the grizzled veterans of the Tartan Army's long war against sobriety and are guaranteed to have no moral worth of any kind. No liver has gone unsacrificed in the search, especially the author's, and the work continues.

There are plainsongs (and fancy ones), as well as sweet and sour ones and every nuance of flavour in between, but they all boil down to the (Completely Unofficial) slogan of the Tartan Army, which is: 'We'll support you evermore, fuck the score!'

The average TA member does not mature until he (or she) has exhausted every other possibility and, with the world and its peoples to be visited at every opportunity, the possibilities are manifold. Whisky is our national drink and another whisky is our national weakness, but we are prepared to try other methods of reaching Nirvana, and I don't mean that mob from Seattle. Singing till you are (dark) blue in the face is one way and I have witnessed the singing of 'Doh-a-Deer' for the duration of an entire match plus the interval. It was against Morocco and much good it did us, as we got gubbed and were out of the World Cup again. But has it stopped us? You know the answer to that one.

We are the Tartan Army, therefore we sing. We drink, therefore we sing. We win (occasionally) therefore we sing. We lose (often) therefore we sing. We sing, sometimes, for no discernible reason.

Now you can do it too.

Ian Black

THE TARTAN ARMY

FOUNDED: SOMETIME IN THE SEVENTIES
NICKNAME: THE TA
BIGGEST WIN AGAINST ENGLAND: 17-0
(MADE THAT ONE UP)
BIGGEST LOSS AGAINST ENGLAND: 3-9
(DIDN'T MAKE THAT ONE UP. WEMBLEY 1961. WAS
THERE. THE SCARS ON MY SOUL WILL NEVER HEAL.)
GROUND: HAMPDEN AND EVERYWHERE ELSE
FANZINE: *HAGGIS SUPPER* (RIP)

*

This was first sung by the Tartan Army in Vienna after an Austrian newspaper commented that the Scots liked to sing: 'And tonight we will hear the sound of music'.

DOH-A-DEER

Doh, a deer, a female deer,
Ray, a drop of golden sun,
Me, a name I call myself,
Fah, a long, long, way to run,

Soh, a needle pulling thread,
Lah, a note to follow soh,
Te, a drink with jam and bread
And that brings us back to doh, oh, oh, oh.

Then repeat until you drop dead or you need another pint, whichever comes first. We sang this for half an hour after we beat England in our last game at Wembley. God knows why, but we don't.

Here's a newer one: it and the next two are from Peter Speed, aka Fringo of the Tartan Army Message Board, henceforth known as the TAMB.

OB-LA-DI OB-LA-DA . . . BERTI VOGTS

Berti had a job in a desert state,
But we said: 'Come to Bonnie Scotland.'
Berti says to Scotland, 'Yes, I cannae wait,'
and we say this as we take him by the hand.

Chorus
Ob-la-di, ob-la-da, Berti Vogts
Oh. Oh oh oh Berti Vogts.
Ob-la-di, ob-la-da, Berti Vogts
Oh. Oh oh oh Berti Vogts.

Berti takes us all out to gay Paree,
This is where it'll all begin.
Leads the team out for all of us to see
and that is when we all begin to sing . . . oh shit!

Chorus

In a couple of years we'll be in Portugal,
The Tartan Army cheering for a win.
Bonnie Scotland banging in the goals
and that is when we all begin to sing:

Chorus

Tune: 'Monkees Theme'

Here we come . . .
stoating down the street . . .
we get the funniest looks
from everyone we meet

Hey, hey we're the TA
and people say we fanny around
but we're too busy singing
to put anybody down

We're just trying to be friendly
we like to sing and play
we're the famous Tartan Army
and we've got something to say

Hey, hey we're the TA
and people say we fanny around
but we're too busy singing
to put anybody down

Peter's songs, and several others from this volume, are now out there in webland. Some of them are even on an official Welcome to Scotland site. Fame at last.

<u>Tune: 'Sailing'</u>

We are drinking,
Always drinking,
Foreign lagers from far away.
Stella Artois,
Whisky and vodka,
We'll be drinking, night and day.

We are singing,
We are singing,
For all the burdz across the sea.
We are singing,
But never minging,
To be with you, to be free.

Can you hear us,
Can you hear us,
Through the dark night far away?
Can you hear us,
Will you cheer us,
To be with you, come what may?

We are Scotland,
Bonnie Scotland,
Always with you across the sea.
We will follow

Through joy and sorrow,
To be near you, to be free.
Oh Lord,
To be near you, to be free.
Oh Lord,
To be near you, to be free.

The Tartan Army Message Board is a relatively recent development, but the TA, like all modern armies, has to be flexible and react to technology positively. It is a disparate and often desperate group of people who, by and large, have two things in common. Each, and this is essential, has access to a computer and the web, and all, apart from a couple of vociferous English critics who post on it, are members of the Tartan Army. The address is www.tartanarmyboard.co.uk. The discussions, jokes, send-ups and arguments that rage on it are fascinating, funny and often furious, and the friendships formed are binding.

There are currently around 3,500 members, but, until fairly recently, ie. the friendly in Paris, only a few had met or knew what the others looked like. One Tamber, as we are known, whose TAMB moniker is Ally Macabre, came up with a cunning plan. A lot of us sent him a few quid and he produced T-shirts with our chosen moniker on the back and the TAMB address on the front. We then met up in Paris and later Aberdeen for an eyeball and more than a few highballs, as well as more than a few high balls from the Scotland team, who in both games were beyond woeful and into truly distressing. More of this later, but in the meantime a new song what my mate Kosmic wrote. Take a deep breath. Optimism is not his middle name.

CROSS, STILL & NATIONALIST

<u>Tune: 'Suite: Judy Blue Eyes'</u>

It's getting to the point,
where Scotland can't score anymore,
We are useless.
Sometimes it hurts so badly inside,
I must cry out loud, 'We're disastrous.'
I am yours, you are mine, we are what we are,
We make it hard!

Remember when we had a football team
that wisnae half bad,
Oh Jim Baxter.
But don't let the past remind us
of what we are not now,
We're useless bastards.
I am yours, you are mine, we are what we are,
We make it hard!

Tearing yourself away frae Craig Brown
you're still not free,
Of incompetence.
Even our best clubs when in Europe
they play like utter mince,
And that's the difference.

I am yours, you are mine, we are what we are,
We make it hard!

Well something inside is telling me
that we've got a problem,
With our tactics.
Skill is the lock and punting the ball is the key,
We play like spastics.
I am yours, you are mine, we are what we are,
We make it hard!

I am yours, you are mine, we are what we are,
We make it hard . . .

Friday evening, settle down to watch Sportscene,
What've I got to lose?
Hazel Irvine prattling guff tae Rob McLean,
This is what we've got to lose.

Can I tell it like it is?
Will ye listen to me laddie?
It's my pride, it's a-suffrin', it's a-dyin',
That's what I've got to lose.

I've got an answer: I'm getting oot ma head,
What've ye got to booze?
Are ye still drinkin' malt whisky wi' Irn Bru?

This is what we've got to lose.

United and Hibernian!
Heart of Midlothian, Caley Thistle
Aberdeen – they're so mean,
Dump them all in the Atlantic.

The Old Firm and the Partick
no wonder that I'm frantic,
Aberdeen they're so mean,
Dump them all in the Atlantic.

Pundits of our nation,
Upon our radio stations, you can hear,
Verbal diarrhoea and mutual masturbation.

Dougie Donnelly, Doo Doo-gie Donnelly, Dougie
Donnelly, Doo Doo-gie Doo.
Dougie Donnelly, Doo Doo-gie Donnelly, Dougie
Donnelly, Doo Doo-gie Doo.
[Jim White, well he just talks shite. Chick Young, well
for that just read hum. Davie Provan sat on Gerry's
McKnee, Dick Donnelly, well he comes frae
Dundee, Archie McP with his eloquent words,
despite the fact that he's a t***.]

Dougie Donnelly, Doo Doo-gie Donnelly, Dougie Donnelly, Doo Doo-gie Doo.
Dougie Donnelly, Doo Doo-gie Donnelly, Dougie Donnelly, Doo Doo-gie Doo.

To return to the TAMB, which has become a tool for seeking help, the telling of jokes, comradeship, character assassinations, arranging gigs and games, vicious slaggings-off, and many other things, including the sharing of pain. Here is one involving the latter, an extract from a thread which I thought worth reproducing. It has even got a couple of songs in it.

ScottyBigDog is a night club steward and his catalogue of job-related injuries is extensive, despite the fact that he is about six and a half feet tall and built like two brick shithouses back to back. This injury wasn't job-related. It really is the way he tells them . . .

* * *

From ScottieBigDog
Just back from the hospital after having suffered an accident.

An accident that most men secretly worry about.

An accident that I wouldnae wish on my worst enemy. Yes, got the auld 'John Thomas' caught in the zipper.

Now, if you've stopped laughing I'll continue. Was at work tonight when I felt the need to pass some water. This went without incident, until it came to the zipping-up part. I put the wee soldier back into the Burtons own-brand boxers (I wouldnae recommend these lads, the button front is lax in its restraint technique) and 'mini-me' popped out as I was ripping up the zip.

Felt the ensuing rush of pain and jerked the zip back down, causing untold amounts of extra damage to my already mangled member. Thought it would be ok at first, as it didnae feel that bad. But became a bit more concerned after seeing the wee pool of blood on the bathroom floor.

(Funny thing though, a poor lad who was standing beside me at the other urinal fell to one knee and his face went white upon seeing the blood splash onto the white porcelain.)

Anywho, ran out to the car and raced like a mad fool to A&E. Slammed the car into a parking space and scarpered inside. Was impressed how well the receptionist managed to stifle her giggles whilst entering my details into the computer, and took a seat in the waiting room.

Shortly guided to a wee treatment room, where several nurses and doctors came through to 'inspect' the wee patient. (Remembering of course folks that it was cold, early in the morning, erm . . . have I said cold? Ach ok, no excuses. It wasn't at its most glorious of lengths.)

Finally, after lying there for about an hour bleeding, a middle-aged Indian doctor arrived who had obviously had just been dragged oota his bed. I think someone said he was a specialist (do you get willy-mangling specialists?).

Anyway, made it my first priority to make this guy my new best friend, as he quite literally held my future in his hands.

After a quick inspection he said that he would stitch it back up, but should it get any worse over time the old '1-2-3-4 skin' will be getting the chop. So, I lay back while I received two local anaesthetic injections into the base of the penis (good God, I nearly backflipped back into the waiting room. Which undoubtedly would have impressed the old lady sitting waiting for her husband), then the stitches.

'So, worked here long?' said SBD in a vain attempt to break the embarrassed silence that was hanging in the air whilst the good doctor, looking very unimpressed, manhandled the meat and two veg.

You know, it's amazing the patterns you see in roofing tiles when you do your damndest not to look at what's happening below.

Anyway, to cut a long story even longer, the doctor

finished off his sewing with a mean-looking cross-stitch, and snipped the thread off. (Can I just add that the snipping noise was not enjoyed either.)

At this point I dared a wee look at the downstairs car crash, and thank the big man I was lying down. Jesus, it looked for all the world like one of those chest bursters from *Aliens*.

Anyway, after a few cautionary words of advice and some pills, a handshake with the doctor signalled my departure from the hospital and my swift journey home in the motor.

Now, the reason I'm telling you all this is three fold.

1. I might as well tell you first, because sure as Santa only comes once a year, someone will find out and post a thread ripping the pish.
2. The missus gets home from her night job in the next hour, so once she hears that any bedroom activity is right out the window for the next couple of weeks, well, this could be my last will and testament. It's been great knowing you all, and spare a thought for me at the next game. Sniff.
3. Part of me finds the whole experience bloody hilarious.

* * *

The replies were not too sympathetic, but empathy obviously played a big part. The weird names are all regular TAMB posters.

*   *   *

From Robbo

I demand SBD name be changed from Scottie-BigDog to ScottieBobbittDog!!!

You will also be getting a bill from Aker-Kvaerner for my PC as I just sprayed coffee all over it and it's starting to smoke!

From Bry fae Thurso

Was anyone else reading this and, knowing SBD, waiting for the punchline??

Anyway, SBD, it could of been worse for the missus – you might have bitten your tongue when you got JT caught.

From Hawkeye Ranoo

Scottie, you're a legend mate, brilliant, but I need tae get this image out of my head. I can see you lying there singing to yourself: 'You are my foreskin my only foreskin. You make me happy when skies are grey, people don't ken how much I stroke you, so please don't take my foreskin away.'

From ScottyBigDog

Cheers for the support all. (Except Robbo. Yer getting yer back door kicked in!)

Now here's the hard part, I'm going for my first toilet visit since the 'incident'. I may be some time.

If I'm not back in five minutes. Just wait longer.

From Hawkeye Ranoo

Let us spray.

From ianblack [me]

Scotty,

Sorry to add to your troubles, mate, but I was laughing so hard that I banged my nose on the keyboard and it started to bleed (my nose, not the keyboard) and translated my entire inbox into Barry Manilow lyrics (it's a very big nose), so my legal beagle will be getting in touch re compen.

Your post is a total and multi-faceted glittering gem and should be preserved for posterity. I will undertake this.

P.S. Could your surgeon sew up nostrils, do you think? And yes, I know it would need to be a really big nose.

From ScottyBigDog

By the way, went for my first pee since the incident

a while ago. The words 'Hot Magma' spring to mind.

From EddieC

Fuck sake, Scotty, that's the best laugh I've had for ages.

I note you omitted to tell us how many stitches it took to repair the old trouser snake. Is that to omit the embarrassment at telling us he sewed up the entire length of it with three stitches?

Serves you right for going home early on Saturday night. I was that dehydrated yesterday I don't think I needed a piss all day.

From ScottyBigDog

Six or seven stitches – to be honest I didn't want to ask as I didn't want to break his concentration!

Apologies for disappearing on Saturday night Ed, the old homing beacon kicked in – must have been a strong beacon 'cause I didn't even get a kebab!

Missus wasn't too impressed with me staggering into the house drunk and doing the 'Fosbury Flop' onto the bed.

From MCTEAGLE

Aye Scottie, and by the sounds of it a 'flop' is all she'll be getting for a while!!

From warwicktartanarmy

Quote: from ScottieBigDog on 12:34 p.m. on 9 June 2003:

'Cheers for the support all (except Robbo. Yer getting yer back door kicked in!). Now here's the hard part, I'm going for my first toilet visit since the "incident". I may be some time.'

I doubt there'll be any 'hard parts' for a while yet young Scottie.

From Robbo

Scottie . . . Ah couldna resist! You have my sympathies and I know how it feels to catch yourself (caught ma luv globes as a youngster, still got a notch or two where the teeth dug in!!) but I also know if it was me who had suffered this injury you would have made ma life a misery every time I turned up to the college and informed all and sundry!!!!

Are you going to be able to work? Though in your line of work it might be dangerous having such an injury . . . don't want the wee man reacting when some bit of totty walks past!!

Just thinking you'll have another party piece to add to your repertoire we saw in that Irish boozer after the game. Now to add to the dislocation of your shoulder and your nose, you can piss in three directions. Simultaneously . . .

But well done for the best post I've seen this year!!

ScottyBigDog

Cheeky bugger, but fair point! Better watch your kilt socks if your standing next to me at the urinals folks.

That's me off work now until at least the weekend. I'm walking about fine, but don't want to risk aggravating the poor wee dingaling.

Cheers, everyone, for the sympathy. To be honest I was prepared to have the 'shiznit' ripped oota me! The only good thing that's come out of it is the swelling, which makes me look like John Holmes (if you don't know who that is, ask to borrow one of your dad's videos from the back of the closet).

Still, the colouration is getting a bit worrying. Stitches are starting to look like a fat bar code.

From warwicktartanarmy

Next time you're in Tesco's ask the girl on the checkout to scan them in, buddy – see how many you get to the pound!

Robbo

Since Big Scott's feeling rather tender let's all sing him a song to make him feel better.

Everyone ready???
[clears throat]
'My ding-a-ling, my ding-a-ling,
who wants to play with my ding-a-ling . . .'

From *AlbaGuBragh*

I know who will not be singing with the rest of us when it comes to '. . . a needle pulling thread'.

ScottyBigDog

And I'll probably avoid, 'We'll be Coming'.
Just watching TV just now, and ironically on came an advert for *Something About Mary*, as it's on ITV2 on Saturday. What was the first clip they showed? The 'zipper' incident. Bastards.

From *Brandantazzle*

ripidydooda ripidydoo

From *ianblack*

Of course, a really evil bastard would be e-mailing Scotty lots of porn. Now, where's that catalogue? Keep your pecker up, Scotty. Or maybe not.

ScottyBigDog

Woke up this morning in a lot of pain.
Why? you may ask. Because my brain seems to

think that 'morning glory' is still an option!
    AARRGGHHH!!

From Tam Ritchie
    It's not like they could leave the stitches a bit loose to compensate for 'morning glory'.

From Gordiewell
    SBD, great story, brilliantly told. It had me in, erm, stitc. . . splitting my sides. Hope you rise to the occasion in the near future. If not, keep hold of any ice lolly sticks. They may come in handy!

From EddieC
    Hot salty water. Last thing you want is gangrene of the boaby.

From Thermopylae
    That reminds me of a joke . . .
    Q. What's green and eats nuts?
    A. Gonorrhoea! [groan]

From Wullg
    My heart goes out to you Scottie. Many years ago, Kawasaki front wheel in tatters = scrotum in tatters. Fifty-seven stitches. I thought I got off light as my pointy bits were undamaged. Everything worked ok

but I remember asking if I would be able to have children and a doctor replying 'Oh aye son, but if I was you I would wait until the stitches come out.'

*   *   *

And that was only part of the thread.

I tidied up the spelling and punctuation here and there, so as not to show people up, as a lot is obviously fired off in the heat of the moment, but you would have thought that an Inverurie man would know how to spell gonorrhoea.

The TAMB is also occasionally the vehicle for a heartfelt plea.

This one is from Weebeastie before the game against Germany. He speaks for me, and for a lot more of us.

*   *   *

Dear Scotland team

Many wouldn't understand the sacrifices I've made to see you play. I've missed my partner's birthday so that I could travel to Poland in March for a 1-1 friendly. I have travelled via plane and train and Lada taxi to Minsk and blagged a transit visa at the border to see you scrape a stunning 0-1 victory. I have taken a fortnight on the sick to spend in French campsites in order to experience World Cup '98 and arrived back to find no job waiting for me.

I have woken up in Berlin train stations, Estonian hotels and Latvian discos with no money in my pocket and a black eye because of you. I have drunk Lithuanian pear cider, Czech pivo, Belarussian vodka and San Marino red wine with a screw top, just to be with you.

I have copped off with Russian beauties and English beasts whilst under your influence and contracted diseases that I can't even pronounce. I have extended the overdraft to get whatever new nasty nylon away shirt you release.

I have sung songs I don't understand to people who don't understand what the song is about. I have abused Jimmy Hill, for reasons that don't make any sense now, but did at the time.

Please, please, please, Scotland. Make me proud once more this weekend.

*　　*　　*

And they did, possibly because a copy of the above was passed to the players before the game.

At the game, a few minutes into the second half, the German fans, not normally the most vociferous or the most offensive, with whom we had a truly brilliant rapport, started chanting: 'Ve hate England, Ve hate England, Ve hate England more than you.'

It was weak at first, but after a few moments they were all at it, and there was a lot of laughter among our troops.

There was then a thoughtful pause as the Tartan Army digested this unusual and unprecedented assertion. Then came the Scots' reply:

'You've only, you've only, you've only fought the bastards twice.'

There is more in this pro-German and anti-English vein to be heard in the TA version of a song titled 'Evil Scotsman'. It isn't a football song and I'm not going to reproduce all the lyrics as some of them are truly offensive, even to me, and that is saying something. PC it is not. One of the milder lines is:

'Just because I wear a skirt don't think I'm fucking gay!'

The song is sung by an uncannily good Billy Connolly soundalike, recorded in, I've been told, a bar in the Balearics. Another couple of lines from it are:

'If you're English or Irish you won't have to die,

But if you're fucking *German* you can kiss your ass goodbye!'

I have now heard this song sung half-a-dozen times or so by different footsoldiers, but I have yet to hear that couplet sung with the nationalities in that order. It now goes:

'If you're *German* or *Irish* you won't have to die,
   But if you're fucking *English* you can kiss your ass
goodbye!'

A nice one from Paddy. He sings it himself.

THE PRAGUE SONG
Lyrics by Patrick Lynch

<u>Tune: The Knock Song by Christy Moore</u>

*A cold and misty mornin' in the summer month o' June
Eight Scottish boys were meetin' up
to drink and sing a tune
On a rusty bus fae London town they headed for the East
Wi' drums, guitars and whistles
and a bevvy for a feast*

*TOORALOO, TOORALAY,
THE TARTAN ARMY'S ON THE PISS
AND ON THE PISS WE'LL STAY*

*The time we got near Dover sure the drink was drunken dry
So the bus hits the hard shoulder
as the traffic all passed by*

'Ahoy there,' shouts the driver, I will sell you cheap
Czech Beer'
Says Peter, gimme forty
'cause I've got a tenner here

TOORALOO, TOORALAY,
THE TARTAN ARMY'S ON THE PISS
AND ON THE PISS WE'LL STAY

The ferry boat was rockin' all the boys were doing a jig
And Alan stripped the willow wi' a granny in a wig
But Fallon took the hurry,
chuckin' pints right down his puss
The pints came back to haunt him
and the smell stank out the bus

TOORALOO, TOORALAY, THE TARTAN
ARMY'S ON THE PISS AND ON THE PISS
WE'LL STAY

When Prague came near the poor bus died
we hitched to our hotel
The hovel we expected looked more like the Taj Mahel
We followed Tricky to the pub to see what we would see
And Simon fainted when he saw the pints were 20p

TOORALOO, TOORALAY,
THE TARTAN ARMY'S ON THE PISS
AND ON THE PISS WE'LL STAY

We took a train up to the hills to see the Juniors game
Wi' T-shirts, shorts and sun specs on,
a sun tan was the aim
Half o Europe sweltrin' on a blisterin' summer's day
Big Colin caught pneumonia
it felt more likeHogmanay

TOORALOO, TOORALAY,
THE TARTAN ARMY'S ON THE PISS
AND ON THE PISS WE'LL STAY

We woke next mornin' early was the day of the big game
Says Russell, if the Scots win things
will never be the same
Six thousand Scots marched up in kilts their heroes for to see
Surprise, the Scots got two goals . . .
but as expected they got three

TOORALOO, TOORALAY,
THE TARTAN ARMY'S ON THE PISS
AND ON THE PISS WE'LL STAY

With heavy hearts we travelled home,
not stayed you may ask why
The truth was that the Tartan Army drank the city dry
At twenty pence a pint, sure it was always going well
Our minds were all in heaven . . . but our livers went to hell

And the classic. It doesn't say what we will do when we arrive.

WE'RE COMING

We're coming, we're coming,
We're coming down the road.
When you hear the noise of the Tartan Army boys,
We'll be coming down the road.

Repeat till your throat needs another beer. You are not drinking for fun, you know.

There is another version of this which was invented in a stress-relieving establishment in Prague, I'm told. Imagine, if youse will, about thirty or forty of the troops singing this as the ladies of the night laugh and clap along, oblivious of the meaning of the words but happy to be sung to:

We'll be coming, we'll be coming
We'll be coming in your face

You can shout and scream
But you'll get the Scottish cream
When we're coming in your face

One for the Auld Enemy. Real shame about our English cousins not winning the World Cup, eh? I was looking forward to hearing about that over and over and over for the next forty-odd years. And it still won't be in colour.

YOU'RE GOING HOME

You're going home, you're going home
England's going home
Three lions on your shirt, two goals in past Seaman
Fifteen pints last night, Beckham's fucking steaming
You're going home, you're going home
England's going home

Incidentally, those lions are actually leopards.

One which arrived in my e-mail within an hour of the end of England's game against Brazil:

His name was Ronaldinho, he was a showman

With a headband on his hair and curls down to there
He would shimmy and do the cha-cha
And while he tried to be a star
England fans cried in Trafalgar
Across a crowded square, they watched as
their team did bore
They were young and they were old
And from their team they wanted more

At the Copa (CO!), Copacabana (Copacabana)
The hottest team won in Shizuka (here)
At the Copa (CO!), Copacabana
Flair and passion were always the fashion
At the Copa . . . Brazil played the game the way it should
be played

(Copa Copacabana)

His name was Seaman, he wore a ponytail
He lined up his wall as he saw Ronaldhino standin' there
And when he finished, he came off his line
But Seaman went a bit too far, the ball sailed over him
and under the bar
And then the punches flew and chairs were
smashed in two
There was blood and a single gun shot
From the English fans back in Crewe

At the Copa (CO!), Copacabana (Copacabana)
The hottest team won in Shizuka (here)
At the Copa (CO!), Copacabana
Flair and passion were always the fashion
At the Copa . . . Brazil played the game the way
it should be played

(Copa . . . Copacabana)
(Copa Copacabana) (Copacabana, ahh ahh ahh ahh)
(Ahh ahh ahh ahh Copa Copacabana)
(Big Tel in the studio is going bananas)
(Flair and passion . . . always the fash–shun)

Latin percussion interlude and dancing around
like madmen . . . madmen who have just
seen England lose.

His name is Ronaldinho, he was a showman
Then in 57 minutes he had to go, but for Brazil this
was not a blow
Now it's a disco, but not in Trafalgar
'Cause it's almost completely empty there
Yes, this defeat was very sare
They sit in pubs so refined, while the Scots drink ourselves
half blind
Their team has lost now and they must come home
Now that Ronaldinho has kicked their behind!

At the Copa (CO!), Copacabana (Copacabana)
The hottest team won in Shizuka (here)
At the Copa (CO!), Copacabana
Flair and passion were always the fashion
At the Copa . . . Brazil played the game the way it should
be played

(Copa) This is what the Scots all love
Copacabana
Copacabana

And another from the same pen fifteen minutes later:

COPACABANNOCKBURN

His name was David,
He was a goalie,
With a pigtail in his hair, why was he standing
way out there?
He tried to run back but couldn't make it,
The Brazilians watched it from afar, as it sneaked
under the bar
You could hear the crowd roar, Rivaldo's lying
on the floor
The lions whimpered out the door,
Oh baby, who could ask for more . . .

At the Copa, oh, Copa-ca-bann-ock-burn,
Its great to watch Rivaldo turn,
At the Copa, oh, Copa-ca-bann-ock-burn,
The man with the moustache should stick to the adverts,
At the Copa – they fell to bits.

His name was Rio, he was a diamond,
He was running round in rings, he saw Rivaldo level
things,
And when he finished, he called him over
But Rio went too slow, Rivaldo slammed it in the goal,
And then Brooking had a spew, Motson bit his mike
in two,
Then Ronaldinho, he got a red card,
But with Mills picked by Sven
It looked like ten versus ten . . .

At the Copa, oh, Copa-ca-bann-ock-burn,
Its great to watch Rivaldo turn,
At the Copa, oh, Copa-ca-bann-ock-burn,
With Heskey near the ball, how did they score a goal
at all?
At the Copa – we laughed and laughed.

His name was Bobby, he was the captain,
But that was forty years ago, that's when they used to
have a go,

Now it's a party, but not for Beckham,
Still in the dress he likes to wear, faded feathers
in his hair.
He slumps down there to unwind and then cries himself
half blind
He lost his cup, and lost his glory,
But up in Scotland, that's not the story . . .

At the Copa, oh, Copa-ca-bann-ock-burn,
Its great to watch Rivaldo turn,
At the Copa, oh, Copa-ca-bann-ock-burn,
Three little kittys on the chest, now we all know who's
the best,
At the Copa . . . we . . . said . . . good-byeeeeeeee!!

denhaagdavid came up with this rhyme later that day.
I don't know if it has a tune.

In a land to the east with a rising sun
The World Cup was there to be won
Countries came from far and wide
To qualify they all tried

Alas the Scots, the Dutch as well
At home, in June they must dwell

But joy the Irish made it there
As did England, after a scare

The opening match in Korean heat
Crushing tackles and nimble feet
France, the champions, masters of all
Somehow fall, to Senegal

France go home early doors
Owen dives and Beckham scores
Argentina out, and Portugal too
England and Ireland both get through

Saturday lunchtime, and it rains
A lucky win against the Danes
Sunday lunchtime a tale of a spot kick
The Spanish score, the Irish are sick

Come the Friday and England stops
All in the pubs, none in the shops
On the telly's that tosser Hansen
If England lose we'll all be dancing

Twenty minutes, a hopeful punt
Owen scores, the little runt
Injury time, blame Ashley Cole
He lets Brazil score a goal

The second half is minutes old
Brazil in blue, not in gold
Ronaldinho thinks he's dreaming
From 35 yards he's just lobbed Seaman

More minutes pass and Mills goes down
Scolari's sitting with a frown
Ten men, thirty minutes left
Are Brazil's hopes to be bereft?

Across the land in homes and bars
Sitting in traffic in their cars
A nation waits for the game to finish
Counting down the last few minutes

The whistle goes, the game is over
Scotland fans, like pigs in clover
Glasses raised and toasts proposed
Who would ever have supposed

Football's finally coming home
Back from the Sapporo dome
Empty-handed and in disgrace
England missed their semi place

Seaman's name is just too good a joke to let go, it would appear. This appeared about 30 seconds after his transfer from Arsenal, sent by Eddie C. He says: 'Oh, to be a headline writer for the *Sun*!!!'

Did Wenger release Seaman prematurely?

Seaman to fill Keegan's box

Wenger wipes Seaman from the Arsenal team sheet

Wenger deposits Seaman into Keegan's lap

Wenger hoping for clean sheets as Seaman shoots up Nnrth

Seaman mess leaves stain on Wenger's managerial record

Seaman fills Schmeichel's shorts

Arsenal fans find Seaman release hard to swallow

Big mess at Highbury as Wenger lets Seaman go

Will Seaman be the new 'flavour of the month' at City?

Wilson: 'No way back, once Seaman released'

City defence pulling together for Seaman

Keegan: 'My desire to succeed needed Seaman'

Wenger: 'I couldn't hold on to Seaman any longer'

Keegan: 'Peter Schmeichel left a hole at the back, I've filled it with Seaman'

So much for the Auld Enema. Here's one for the Auld Alliance:

GAY PAREE

Gay Paree, gay Paree,
We're the famous Tartan Army,
And we're off to gay Paree

Replace 'gay Paree' with name of ground (e.g. Wemb-allee), city or country being visited, which is difficult to do with places like the Faroe Isles or Iceland, I admit, but get on with it. Do you want to be a foot soldier or not?

On the same theme . . .

Que sera, sera,
Whatever will be will be,
We're going to gay Paree,
Que sera, sera

And when we got there we were singing, to the tune of 'Pierre', courtesy of a TAMB member called Sacks, aka Steve Ricketts:

Biere
Je veux encore une biere
Je parade mon derriere
Garcon, encore une biere.

We were also singing, at half-time, after the French had given us a football lesson and were winning 4-0

We're gonny win 5-4
We're gonny win 5-4

On the train on the way back into Paris some benighted souls were singing, to the tune of 'Those Were the Days My Friend':

They couldny make it six
They couldny make it six

There are various manifestations of this acceptance of the vagaries of fate. In Prague, after we had surrendered a 2-0 lead and had lost 3-2

Two-nil . . . and we fucked it up

The above was also heard at the home game against Belgium, when we lost a goal with .00005 of a millisecond to go.

Then we sing, and we mean it:

YOU ARE MY SCOTLAND

You are my Scotland
My bonnie Scotland
You make me happy when skies are grey
You'll never know how
Much we love you
Please don't take my Scotland away

Even the soft drink imbibers are patriotic:

We hate Coca-Cola
We hate Fanta too . . . it's shite!
For we're the Tartan Army
and we drink Irn Bru

There is a less insulting version:

We hate Coca-Cola
We hate Fanta too . . . and Sprite!
For we're the Tartan Army
and we drink Irn Bru

And an alcoholic one:

> *We hate Coca-Cola*
> *We hate Fanta too . . . and Sprite!*
> *For we drink Eldorado*
> *Mixed with Irn Bru*

All of these soft drinks are of course not shite, but reputable products, or so I'm told, as I have no personal experience of soft drinks.

HERE WE GO

> *Here we go*
> *Here we go*
> *Here we go*
> *Here we go*
> *Here we go*
> *Here we go*
> *Here we go*
> *Here we go*
> *Here we go*
> *Here we go*

and so on. Do you think that you will remember the words?

WE'RE AT THE TOP OF THE TABLE

We're at the top of the table
Looking down on Croatia
And the only explanation I can find
Is that man Neil McCann
I've always been a fan
'Cause he's put us at the top of the table

Sung by the Inverness Boys after the France home match, March 2000:

Tune: 'Bless Them All'

Goodnight Horse
Goodnight Horse
I'll say goodnight to my horse
And as I'm saying goodnight to my horse
I'll say goodnight to my horse

(Repeat until shouted at)

Heard in the back streets of Prague, June 1999:

Czech Repub
Czech Repub

We're the famous Tartan Army
And we're here to check the pubs

An established classic, donated by Wee John of the Perthshire Tartan Army, though I believe Tam Coyle of the West of Scotland TA had some input.

DRINK AROUND THE CLOCK

When the clock strikes 1, 2 & 3
15 pints and they're all for me

Chorus
We're gonna drink around the clock tonight
We're gonna drink, drink, drink till broad daylight,
We're gonna drink, gonna drink around the clock tonight
Shooby doo, shooby doo, shooby doo doo doo

When the clock strikes 4, 5 & 6
wur off the pints and wur ontae nips

Chorus

When the clock strikes 7, 8 & 9
wur off the nips and wur ontae wine

Chorus

When the clock strikes 10, 11, 12
Well Ah'm awright and how's yersel?

(You must shake someone's hand at this point)

Wur gonna drink, gonna drink around the clock tonight
Shooby doo, shooby doo

Heard in San Marino, October 2000:

Show me the way to San Marino
Lots of beer and lots of vino
I'm dreaming of two to zero
And Hamann scored for Germany
La-la-laa-la-la-la, Hamann,
La-la-laa-la-la-la, Hamann,
La-la-laa-la-la-la
And Hamann scored for Germany

First heard in San Marino, this became an anthem in Croatia:

Tune: 'That's Amore'

When the thing hits the thing
It's a big fucking thing
It's a thingy

For our southern cousins, in memory of 1977, and to celebrate the Silver Jubilee of the occasion:

Tune: 'You Are My Sunshine'

We stole your goalposts
Your only goalposts
We stole your goalposts
And your pitch too
You never knew how much you'd miss them
Until we took your goalposts away

And for them in Japan and South Korea:

There's only one South Korea
Where you get diarrhoea
Walkin' along with your dog in your wok
Walkin' in a nuclear wasteland

Arriving at the airport in Poland:

We're the famous Tartan Army and we've all got
foot 'n' mouth . . . foot 'n' mouth . . .

And at the game:

What's it like to queue for bread?

From that bonnie fechter, Alan Breck, of the TAMB:

We had an unusual tale at Italia 90 where Gordon Banks
sat in front of us at the Brazil game. Only for comments such
as: 'Watch that fuckin flagpole – it could take someone's eye
oot!' to emerge from the TA ranks.

And the complete history of a chant from gordonjj of
the TAMB:

On the way to Estonia I got the ferry from Stockholm.
When I booked it from there the girl in the tourist info said
to me that the ferry left at 6 o'clock and arrived at 8.30, so
I went ahead. After arriving in Stockholm I then realised it
was 8.30 in the effin morning, fourteen and a half hours. I
was gobsmacked, and the thought of going that way home
was really getting to me (putting it politely) so I managed to
blag my way on to an Estonia airways flight for £120 from

Tallinn to Glasgow along with all the lads. Being slightly intoxicated on arrival to the aircraft, and I mean slightly, I asked the stewardess if I could speak to the pilot. She agreed and when I went to the cockpit I was sat down behind the captain. There were three seats in the cockpit so I politely asked if I could sit there for the whole flight and after about twenty seconds' discussion with the co-pilot they agreed it would be ok, so there I was in the cockpit for the whole duration of the flight, with stewardesses bringing in my drinks and duty free. What an experience.

After the plane stopped at Glasgow I emerged from the cockpit to a chorus of:

> *He's the captain of the plane (of the plane)*
> *He's the captain of the plane (of the plane)*
> *You're mental and your barmy*
> *You're in the Tartan Army*
> *You're the captain of the plane*

Gordon now calls himself The Tartan Paratrooper, as he jumped out of a plane for a TAMB charity.

Alternative 'Doh-a-Deer':

> *Jim Leighton is number one,*
> *Calderwood is number two,*
> *Tommy Boyd is number three,*

Colin Hendry never fails,
Gordon Durie's on the ball,
Gallagher's about to score,
Johnny Collins scores a goal,
AND BURLEY'S B-A-G-G-I-O.

In Belarus:

> *Here we glow, here we glow, here we glow.*

And now, a world premiere. The first official printing of The Ally Maciver oevre, tara!

COME NOW! GATHER NOW!
(Tune: 'The Roses O' Prince Charlie'
– Ronnie Browne)

Chorus
Come now! Gather now!
Here whaur the Saltires blaw
Proud is the Lion Rampant stitched on my chest
Here now! Scotland calls!
We'll stand and we will roar
We'll stand up and we'll cheer for Bonnie Scotland

1.

Raise yer glass in the Iron Horse
Yer bonnie pint tae wield

Stand by yer grandsires
On Wembley's battered field
Or the terraces o' Hampden
Yer courie weans tae shield
We'll stand up and we'll cheer for Bonnie Scotland
Come now . . .

2.

We drink spirits, wine and lager
In far and distant lands
We're ayeways makin' new friends
We're ayeways shakin' hands
Return seldom in glory
But we don't give a damn
We'll stand up and we'll cheer for Bonnie Scotland
Come now . . .

3.

Tak yer strength fae the field man
Whaur Baxter scored his goals
The ships on the Clyde heard
A nation stir its soul
The water o' life toasted
Keegan on the Dole
Hand of God and Pearce's penalty man!
Come now . . .

TARTAN BARMY

(Tune: 'Bonnie Dundee')

Chorus

Come lift up your cup, come lift up your can,
Resplendent in tartan every loyal fan,
We travel the world and we drink the pubs dry,
Oh there's no-one quite like us, we're Scots you and I.

1.

There are some think we're crazy, there's some think
we're daft,
But win lose or draw we will have the last laugh,
We will never forsake you, back you to the hilt,
With a skirl o' the pipes and a swing o' the kilt.

Chorus

2.

So dust down your bunnet and buckle your belt,
Lace your brogues tightly and straighten your kilt,
For there's beer to be drunk, there are songs to be sung,
Reputation precedes us, the night is yet young.

Chorus

3.

The thistle's our flower, the saltire our flag,
Our lion stands rampant, there's only one snag,
We're better at drinking than kicking a ball,
Oh we're everyone's friends but we'll ne'er win . . . at all.

Chorus

4.

So wherever you wander be sure and stand tall,
Keep a smile and a handshake to greet one and all,
And whatever befalls us there's one thing that's sure,
We're all Tartan Barmy and there is no cure.

Chorus

WHEN WE WON AT WEMBLEY

(Tune: 'MacPherson's Rant')

Well England thought that they were the best
Back in 1967
But Baxter and Law were the best you ever saw
And we were in seventh heaven
Sae wontonly, sae dauntinly

And sae gallusly gae'd we
We sang our songs and we danced around
When we won at Wembley

Ten years on their hurt had nearly gone
T'was time to inflict more pain
We stole their pitch and their goalposts
And they've never been seen again
Sae wontonly, sae dauntinly
And sae gallusly gae'd we
We sang our songs and we danced around
When we won at Wembley

And now it's time for England to build a new home
Sad Wembley is fallin down
They wanted to finish with a victory
But along came Craigie Brown
Sae wontonly, sae dauntinly
And sae gallusly gae'd we
We sang our songs and we danced around
When we won at Wembley

JEAN PAUL WHAUR'S YER BOOZERS?

Let the wind blow high let the wind blow low
'Round gay Paree in our kilts we'll go
And all we ever want to know is
Jean Paul whaur's yer boozers?

Well there's some o' us frae the Isle of Skye
Some fae the Lowlands some fae the High
We've a terrible thirst and we don't know why
Jean Paul whaur's yer boozers?

We drink wine and we drink gin
Vodka, beer frae a bottle or a tin
Breakfast we'll start o'er again
Jean Paul whaur's yer boozers?

We've been tae Rome, we've been tae France
We'll be aff tae Lisbon ge'en hawf a chance
We like a drink an' we don't wear pants
Jean Paul whaur's yer boozers?

Ah've goat ma ticket an' Ah've goat my flag
Ah've a clean spare T-shirt in my bag
Now all I need is a beer an' a . . . shave
Jean Paul whaur's yer boozers?

I WILL GO

Chorus
I will go, I will go
When the football is over
Tae the square wi' the pubs
I'm a Tartan Army soldier
I will go, I will go

When the big game comes along
We all get taegither
'Cos we're braw Scottish lads
In wur kilts and wur feathers
I will go, I will go

Chorus

Well we all climbed aboard
Wi' the carry oots we're bringing
You could hear us all around
When the troops started singing
I will go, I will go

Chorus

When we landed at the airport
And saw the foreign ladies

We knew that some would fall
And some stay to make babies
I will go, I will go

Chorus

I've a Lion on my chest
A hip flask in my sporran
And underneath my kilt
Absolutely nothing's worn
I will go, I will go

Chorus

When we cam back tae the pub
All the beer barrels were empty
Wee John had missed the gemme
But we left him there wi' plenty
I will go, I will go

Chorus

TWA TARTAN ARMY LADS

(orig. 'Twa Recruitin Sergeants')

And it's oot o' the taxis and intae aeroplanes
Cross-channel ferries and overnight trains
Get a feather tae yer bunnet, a kilt abune yer knee
Enlist bonnie laddie and come awa wi' me

Twa Tartan Army lads cam down by oor inn
Wi' stories and songs 'bout the places they'd been
They gave us such a laugh it brought a tear tae the eye
And they didnae leave until they drank the place dry

And it's oot o' the taxis . . .

We decided there and then that we would enlist
Cos we like tae sing songs and we like tae get . . . kissed
We sent aff wur photies tae the SFA
Noo wi' kilts, flags an tammies we're all on oor way

And it's oot o' the taxis . . .

Now we've friends out in Poland and friends in Bordeaux
Zagreb, Prague and Riga and Sarajevo
Arnhem and Bremen, Tallinn and Rimini
The only place we're no welcome is down by Wemballey

And it's oot o' the taxis . . .

But noo oor day is comin', the clock's tickin' down
You'd best get prepared or else no hang around
We're gaun for independence and we just cannae wait
Cos Jack McConnell fucked up Scotland Two Thousand
and Eight!

And it's oot o' the taxis . . .

And now our day is coming, we're a' makin plans
In Germany and Iceland there will be ten thousand fans!
Nobody will stop us. The world will hear us roar
When the Tartan Army march on Euro Two Thousand
and Four!

And it's oot o' the taxis . . .

HAMPDEN PARK-E-O
(orig. 'Killiecrankie-o')

Whaur ha' ye been sae braw lad?
Whaur ha' ye been in yer kiltie-o?
Whaur ha' ye been sae braw lad?
Cam' ye by Hampden Park-e-o?

Chorus
An' ye had been whaur I hae been
Ye wadna been sae sober-o
An' ye had sung what I hae sung
On the terraces o' Hampden Park-e-o

I hae drank on land, I hae drank at sea
At hame I drank wi' my auntie-o
Then I sang wi' piss heads fae Dundee
On the terraces o' Hampden Park-e-o
An' ye had been . . .

Chorus

The bauld Berti hae joined oor troops
On the road tae Portugal-e-o
He's brought us pride, and we're a' richt gled
An' we'll sing tae him at Hampden Park-e-o
An' ye had been . . .

Chorus

Sven Erikson, whit a Swedish farce
Tae sell his soul tae the English-o
Ye'd better kiss'd ma braw fat arse
Than come tae Hampden Park-e-o
An' ye had been . . .

Chorus

It's nae shame, it's nae shame
It's nae shame tae boak-e-o
There's sour drunks hae sprayed their chunks
On the terraces o' Hampden Park -e-o
An' ye had been . . .

LEEZIE LINDSEY

Will ye gang tae the fitba' Leezie Lindsey?
Will ye gang tae the fitba' wi' me?
Will ye gang tae the fitba' Leezie Lindsey?
An help me tae cheer oan ma team

Well tae gang tae the fitba' wi' you sir
I dinna ken how that may be
For I ken nae the team that ye follow
Nor ken I the lad I'm goan wi

Will ye gang . . .

Oh Leezie Lass ye maun ken little
If ye say ye dinna ken me
For I'm part o' Scotland's Tartan Army
We're supporters o' high degree

Will ye gang . . .

Now she's a kilt an a shirt o' blue satin
An she's goanae huv a drink or three
For she's aff wi' Scotland's Tartan Army
Tae help them tae cheer on the team

Will ye gang . . .

Ally nicked the chorus for this next one from Ian Adie of *Scotland Be Good* and *The Wee'est Pipe Band in the World* fame. He couldn't remember where he'd heard it.

THE TARTAN ROVER

We've travelled with Scotland for many a year
And the memories and journeys we'll always hold dear
And now we are ready to travel once more
And we'll all have a party whatever the score

And it's planes, trains and taxis
We'll be there on the day
To watch Bonnie Scotland
Wherever they play

You'll see us arriving in twos, threes or fours
At the airports, train stations, hotels and harbours
Then it's off to the main square, the fountains, the bars
We don't even check in 'til we've had twenty jars

And it's planes, trains and taxis . . .

We take over the town but the locals don't care
'Cos they're all asking questions about underwear

Is it true what they say? Gie's a flash o' yer bum!
Then they're wantin' to tak ye awa hame tae
meet Mum . . .

And it's planes, trains and taxis . . .

Now the English don't like it, they don't understand
They think our good humour's a bit underhand
But the truth is we just like a beer and a song
With a smile and a handshake you'll no' go far wrong

And it's planes, trains and taxis . . .

Oh yes it's the life o' a traveller for me
I'll follow Bonnie Scotland 'til I'm eighty-three
We may seldom win, but here's one to confuse
No matter the score we know we'll never lose

And it's planes, trains and taxis . . . x2

Is Alasdair Maciver brilliant or what? Buy him a beer
if you ever meet him, and I'll pay you back.
In his honour:

ALLY'S ARMY

We're on the drugs with Ally's Army
We're all taking Benzedrine
And we'll really shake them up
When we drink it out of a cup
'Cos Scotland are the greatest football team

And his response. This is a man who knows a thing or three about the subject, whether from the inside or the outside, I know not. He claims to have found this on the web.

He says: 'Absolutely no idea what this Benzedrine stuff is, so did a wee search and found a new song for you . . . (fifth day is the one!).'

MY PDOC

On the first day of Christmas my pdoc gave to me
A dx of insanity

On the second day of Christmas my pdoc gave to me
Two caps of lithium
Which made both of my hands all shaky

On the third day of Christmas my pdoc gave to me
Three puvules Prozac

Two caps of lithium
And now I can barely see

On the fourth day of Christmas my pdoc gave to me
Four hits of Zoloft
Three pills called Prozac
Two caps of lithium
Now my mouth tastes like soiled undies

On the fifth day of Christmas my pdoc gave to me
Five Benzedrine.
Four hits of Zoloft
Three puvules Prozac
Two caps of lithium
I will never pay off that shopping spree

On the sixth day of Christmas my pdoc gave to me
Six caps of Dalmane
Five Benzedrine.
Four hits of Zoloft
Three puvules Prozac
Two caps of lithium
Whoa, my feet feel so awful heavy

On the seventh day of Christmas my pdoc gave to me
Seven tabs of Hadol
Six caps of Dalmane

Five Benzedrine.
Four hits of Zoloft
Three puvules Prozac
Two caps of lithium
I'm becoming a lock-jawed zombie

On the eighth day of Christmas my pdoc gave to me
Eight wedges Serzone
Seven tabs of Hadol
Six caps of Dalmane
Five Benzedrine.
Four hits of Zoloft
Three puvlules Prozac
Two caps of lithium
Oh, my head is so sore and dizzy

On the ninth day of Christmas my pdoc gave to me
Nine doses Nardil
Eight wedges Serzone
Seven tabs of Hadol
Six caps of Dalmane
Five Benzedrine.
Four hits of Zoloft
Three puvlules Prozac
Two caps of lithium
A tub of water and I'm still thirsty

On the tenth day of Christmas my pdoc gave to me
Ten more Effexor
Nine doses Nardil
Eight wedges Serzone
Seven tabs of Hadol
Six caps of Dalmane
Five Benzedrine.
Four hits of Zoloft
Three puvlules Prozac
Two caps of lithium
Now all I can do is just pee

On the eleventh day of Christmas my pdoc gave to me
Eleven Paxil dancing
Ten more Effexor
Nine doses Nardil
Eight wedges Serzone
Seven tabs of Hadol
Six caps of Dalmane
Five Benzedrine.
Four hits of Zoloft
Three puvlules Prozac
Two caps of lithium
I just know he is out to get me

There was a lot more about various drugs but I think
I'll stick with the alcohol.

Here is Ian and Alan Adie's original version, which they recorded before the '98 World Cup. Thanks to them for permission to use it and to Ian for the next one. 'Scotland be Good' is surely the most joyful and exuberant call to arms that any army has ever enjoyed. Ian is the wee blue-faced barra in the Viking helmet on the front of my book *Tales of the Tartan Army*. If you meet him, get him to tell you about how he got Chuck Berry's go-ahead to use the tune.

TARTAN ARMY TRAVELS
Tune: 'The Wild Rover'

We've travelled with Scotland for many a year
And the memories and journeys we will ever hold dear
And now we are ready to travel once more
To the stadiums of France to see the Scots score

Chorus
And by plane, train or taxi
(C'mon ye Scots!)
We'll be there on the day
To see Bonny Scotland wherever they play

We started in Germany in '74
'78 was Argentina we supported once more

'82 saw us suntanned and drinking in Spain
'86 on to Mexico, tequila again

Chorus

To Italy in '90 where the weather was fine
'92 was in Sweden where the Scots fans did shine
We out-sang, we out-danced, we out-shone the rest
And that's why Scots supporters were voted the best

Chorus

We missed dear America in '94
'96 against England . . . we'll say no more
Now here is a message to the good folks of France
Come join the Tartan Army for a song and a dance

Chorus

SCOTLAND BE GOOD
Tune: 'Johnny B. Goode'

*Way up in Bonnie Scotland there's a football team
The greatest Scots eleven that there's ever been
They're going to France in '98 to score some goals
We're going to sing and dance and do some Jock 'n' roll
The French, the Dutch, the Germans passing by will say
Hey my my yeah, the Scots can play*

*I said go! Go Bonnie Scotland go! Go Bonnie Scotland go!
Go Bonnie Scotland go! Go, go, go!
Scotland be good*

*We're jamming with Jamaicans on the beaches of France
Showing them the rhythms of the Tartan Army dance
The boys from Brazil are doing the samba
Listening to the tune of the Mexican 'La Bamba'
The Tartan Army boys are getting ready to rave
As the bagpipes are playing 'Scotland the Brave'
I said go! Go Bonnie Scotland go! Scotland be good!*

*I said go! Go Bonnie Scotland go! Go Bonnie Scotland go!
Go Bonnie Scotland go! Go, go, go!
Scotland be good*

We made it to the final and it's going to be great
The greatest Scots eleven can hardly wait
They've made a solemn promise to the Tartan Army boys
We're gonny win the cup and then we'll make some noise
The football nations of the world will stop and say
Hey my my yeah, the Scots can play

I said go! Go Bonnie Scotland go! Go Bonnie Scotland go!
Go Bonnie Scotland go! Go, go, go!
Scotland be good

ARGENTINA CHANT

(In reference to Argentina beating England)

Ar-Gen-Tina
Ar-Gen-tina
Ar-Gen-Tina

and so on

STAND UP IF YOU HATE ENGLAND

Stand up if you hate England
Stand up if you hate England
Stand up if you hate England

Sit down if you hate England
Sit down if you hate England
Sit down if you hate England
Sit down if you hate England

Dance around if you hate England
Dance around if you hate England
Dance around if you hate England
Dance around if you hate England

IF YOU WANT TO GO TO HEAVEN WHEN YOU DIE

If you want to go tae heaven when ye die
You must wear a Scottish scarf or a tie
You must wear a Scottish bonnet
With 'Fuck the English' on it
If ye want to go to heaven when you die

WEMBELEE

Wembelee, Wembelee,
Was the finest pitch in Europe till we took it all away,
Wembelee . . .

CHEER UP KEVIN KEEGAN

Cheer up Kevin Keegan
Oh what can it mean
To a sad English bastard
And a shite football team

I have seen versions of the following in thirty-one languages, including Gaelic, Sanskrit and Hebrew. You can access it on the web at *sadbasturdsarus*. I've met Jimmy Hill and he likes Scotland. Shame about that 'toepoke' line, which I shall personally inscribe on his tombstone, if I live that long.

NOUS DÉTESTONS JIMMY HILL

Nous détestons Jimmy Hill
Il est un p***
Il est un p***

We hate Jimmy Hill
He's a p***
He's a p***

And he isn't gay in any sense of the word.

After a conversation in the pub with a chum of mine, Ken McCluskey (of the famous McCluskey Brothers, said the name dropper) regarding the above song, the etymology of the Scottish word 'dauner' or 'daunder', and various other stuff, as you do in the pub, Ken sent me this one. As far as I know, we are the only people who have ever sung it, but I think that it might catch on. The McCluskey Brothers' latest album is a compilation of their greatest hits. It is called *Housewife's Choice* and can (and should) be obtained from Linn Records.

Tune: The Happy Wanderer

I love to go a daundering
down by the Glasgow Green
It was there I met old Jimmy Hill
The famous English Queen

He's a poof. He's a poof. He's a poo-oo-oo-oo-oo-oo-oo-oo-f.
He's a poof. He's a poof. Oh, Jimmy Hill's a poof.

With his pointy chin
and Saxon ways
You know he looks quite scary
We talked of a roasting night in Seville
And that toe-poke by David Narey

He's a poof . . .

In by-gone days at Coventry
Jimmy raised the roof
But now retired
not quite expired
Jimmy's still a poof

He's a poof . . .

Now all foot soldiers
lend an ear
listen what I say
If you chance to meet old Jimmy Hill
Watch your back . . . he's gay.

He's a poof . . .

It really is a shame that he isn't. Do you think if he
was, that we would sing:
    'He's a straight . . .?

From Saltire of the TAMB, after a discussion about the boringness of the Jimmy Hill song, another suggestion, and one that we can't get sued for:

We hate Jonathan King
Paedophile, paedophile

And from New Model Tartan Army, a more forgiving first line, but with a sting in the tail:

We don't mind Jimmy Hill,
He's still a poof . . .

IF I HAD THE WINGS OF AN EAGLE

If I had the wings of a eagle
And the great big arse of a crow
I'd fly over what used to be Wembley tomorrow
And shite on the bastards below, below
Shite on
Shite on
Shite on the bastards below
Shite on
Shite on
Shite on the bastards below

The national anthem. Personally I prefer Hamish Henderson's 'Freedom Come All Ye' and recently I am inclining to 'Auld Lang Syne', but this is what we sing. Thanks to Ronnie Browne for permission to print it here.

FLOWER OF SCOTLAND

O Flower of Scotland
When will we see
Your like again
That fought and died for
Your wee bit hill and glen
And stood against him
Proud Edward's army
And sent him homeward
Tae think again.

The hills are bare now
And autumn leaves lie thick and still
Oe'r land that is lost now
Which those so dearly held
That stood against him
Proud Edward's army
And sent him homeward
Tae think again.

Those days are past now
And in the past they must remain
But we can still rise now
And be the nation again
That stood against him
Proud Edward's army
And sent him homeward
Tae think again.

We have to have something from Rabbie, the prototype Tartan Army foot soldier. Everybody thinks of it as a dirge, but when I sing it I give it laldy and the words stiffen my spine and pull my shoulders back as I look the world squarely in the face. I am a Scot and damn proud of it. We produced Robert Burns, the man who gave the world the concept that a man's a man for a' that. That is something to hold your head high about.

SCOTS WHA HAE

Scots, wha hae wi' Wallace bled
Scots, wham Bruce has aften led
Welcome to your gory bed
Or to victorie!

Now's the day, and now's the hour
See the front o' battle lour
See approach proud Edward's power
Chains and slaverie!

Wha will be a traitor knave?
Wha can fill a coward's grave?
Wha sae base as be a slave?
Let him turn and flee.

Wha for Scotland's King and law
Freedom's sword will strongly draw
Freeman stand, or freeman fa'?
Let him follow me!

By oppression's woes and pains!
By your sons in servile chains!
We will drain our dearest veins
But we shall be free!

Lay the proud usurpers low!
Tyrants fall in every foe!
Liberty's in every blow!
Let us do – or dee!

Here's a song about another Scottish hero.

There is a group of people in Argentina called the Diegorian Brotherhood who have set up The Church of the Hand of God. They have their own calendar and it is currently 42AD . . . the AD meaning After Diego. They celebrate Christmas on his birthday and their bible is his autobiography, *I Am Diego*. I swear that I am not making any of this up.

They also have their own Ten Commandments, which include: 'You will only be a fan of Maradona and not any football club in particular.' They celebrate 22 June as International Hand of God Day. It is the anniversary of him scoring against England in the quarter final of the 1986 World Cup.

On that day in 2003 I got to go into the BBC studio in Glasgow and sing this song on BBC Scotland for a bunch of English fans in London. I shouted the 'Out! Out! Out!' with every fibre of my being. And I got paid for it. Life is very, very sweet sometimes.

THE MARADONA

You put your left hand in,
You put your left hand out,
You put your left hand in and you shake it all about,
You do the Maradona and you score a goal,
That's what it's all about.

Oh! Diego Maradona!
Oh! Diego Maradona!
Oh! Diego Maradona!
He put the English Out! Out! Out!

Here's an alternative one for Tommy Brolin, of Sweden, who also assisted us in that dark delight called Schadenfreude.

THE TOMMY BROLIN

You put your left leg in
You put your left leg out
in out in out and shake it all about
You do the Tommy Brolin and you turn around
That's what it's all about.
Oh! Tommy, Tommy Brolin
Oh! Tommy, Tommy Brolin
Oh! Tommy, Tommy Brolin
He put the English out! Out! Out!

CHEESE AND BISCUITS

We love cheese and biscuits,
We love horsemeat too,
We love Michel Platini,
La France we love you.

An alternative version of this is . . .

> *We love Brigitte Bardot,*
> *We love champagne too,*
> *We love Michel Platini,*
> *Les Français we love you.*

And in Belgium:

> *We love Hercule Poirot,*
> *We love Tintin too,*
> *We love Re-ené Magritte,*
> *And Belgium we love you.*

Sweden away qualifier:

> *We love Saab motors,*
> *Ingmar Bergman too,*
> *We love Abba and porno,*
> *And Sweden we love you.*

For the Danish:

> *We love Danish bacon,*
> *We love Carlsberg too,*
> *We love Hans Christian Anderson,*
> *And Denmark we love you!*

And when they beat us in Mexico:
You can stick your streaky bacon up your arse!

More words of encouragement for other countries:

We love Gauchos and Incas,
We love Diego too (he's GREAT!),
We love Eva Perón,
And Argentina we love you.

EVERYWHERE WE GO

Everywhere we go
People want to know
Who the hell we are
So we're gonna tell them
We're the Tartan Army
We're mental and we're barmy

Ooooooh, ooooooh, oooh
Scotland (nanananana)
Scotland
We'd walk a million miles
For one of your goals . . .
(and a barbershop quartet or octet or whatever sings . . .)
You sometimes have to!
Oh Scotland

This song is copyright of George Ewen. If you want to sing it, get in touch with George, wherever he is. He will provide you with music and all that technical stuff.

THE COLOURS OF SCOTLAND

We sing of the land we are happy is ours,
From the Borders on through to Orkney and Shetland,
Greeting the Lowlands and Highlands, along
With all the Hebrides.

SCOTLAND, O SCOTLAND,
Your 'FLOWER' is blooming from mountain to shore.
SCOTLAND, O SCOTLAND,
We will gladly praise your beauty evermore.
We'll thrill to the wind off the sea on our face
When we sail for France with the Tartan Army,
Cheering our country and raising our team
To play as soccer's best.

SCOTLAND, O SCOTLAND,
As loyal supporters our pride is your name.
SCOTLAND, O SCOTLAND,
On and off the field we'll play a bonny game.
We'll welcome the hour and the challenge it brings
With a Wallace heart in a brave endeavour,

Lifting our spirits, as facing our flag
We pledge to give our all.

SCOTLAND, O SCOTLAND,
The lion is Rampant, the Saltire is blest.
SCOTLAND, O SCOTLAND,
'LET US DO' with valour in a fair contest.

SCOTLAND, O SCOTLAND,
The red on the yellow, or the white cross on the blue,
SCOTLAND, O SCOTLAND,
We will strive to win the day and honour you.

This is one for our Norwegian chums.

SING WHEN YOU'RE WHALING

Sing when you're whaling,
You only sing when you're whaling,
Sing when you're whaling,
You only sing when you're whaling.

And this one is from the first game in the Faroes, when Andy MacArthur, foot soldier supreme, marched off the ferry in good order along with his comrades-in-arms, each of them brandishing a blow-up whale, complete with wee kilts and tartan scarves. Even the Faroese laughed, but it took a while. It's a sensitive subject.

SAVE THE WHALES

Save the whales,
Save the whales,
We're the famous Tartan Army
And we're here to save the whales.

In France this became both:

Save the snails!
Save the snails!
We're the famous Tartan Army
And we're here to save the snails.

And, from some Glaswegian gastrognomes of Zurich:

Eat the snails!
Eat the snails!
We're the famous Tartan Army
And we're here to eat the snails.

And a new one from our latest near-disaster in the Faroes.

PUFFIN' DOWN THE FJORD
(Heard on the *Dambusters*-style landing
at Soravagur Airport, Faroe Islands)

We're puffin' . . .
We're puffin' . . .
We're puffin' down the fjord,
When you hear the noise of the Tartan Army boys
We'll be puffin' down the fjord

This is a reaction to the way that the plane approaches the airport. It skims over the fjord at what seems like wave-height, then, just as the cliff is about to smash you into a micron-thick layer of protoplasm, the plane heaves itself up and sort of pancakes on the runway. Very scary biscuits indeed. When you get there they stamp your passport with the word 'Komin'. I wasn't the only one singing:

Komin, Komin, it's nice tae see ye.

And back in Paris.

<u>Tune: 'Juantanamera'</u>

Only a pylon, it's just a big fuckin pylon,
only a pylon,
The Eiffel's only a pylon.

Why, incidentally, is there only Juantanamera?

MAIR SCHADENFREUDE

Southgate missed a penalty, Southgate missed a penalty
Ha ha ha. Ha ha ha.

Brother Batty, Brother Batty,
Missez-vous, missez-vous,
Sunny Argentina, sunny Argentina,
Ha ha ha, ha ha ha.

I heard this for the first time as we made our way to
the ground for the Scotland/Brazil match that kicked
off the 1998 World Cup.

This next has been kicking around on the web for ages. I don't know who wrote it, but I laugh every time I read it. It is the opening game of the 1998 World Cup.

We take up the action in the third minute of the first half . . .

Leighton: Let's huv a name on this, I don't want tae see the baw here again for at least another twenty seconds.

Lambert: Shit, it's coming towards me. Whit the fuck dae Ah dae wi' it noo?

Durie: Don't fuckin' pass it here, ya donkey, I dinna want it. Gie it to Jackson.

Jackson: Shit, wasn't expecting it this early in the game. I think I'll gie it back tae Paul.

Lambert: No' again.

Boyd: Fuck off Lambert, gie it tae Burley, he'll know whit tae dae.

Burley: Ach, that's miles away, Tam.

Collins: That's come to me nicely. How am I looking?

Fantastic I bet. These Brazilians are pish by the way, looking good Johnny Boy, Ah can skin them all. Shit, lost it. Hope the camera didn't get that one.

Calderwood: Christ, he's comin' at me, where's Colin? Colin, get ower here, that silky bastard Ronaldo's comin' for me. Whit noo?

Hendry: Slide him.

Calderwood: Whit?

Hendry: Leave him tae me . . . fuck, missed him the wee shite.

Leighton: Oh for fuck's sake.

Dailly: Better get back.

Gallacher: Wonder what's happening up there? Oh, corner to Brazil. Better go and stand next tae somebody.

Leighton: Who's on Sampaio?

Jackson: Are we eating out tonight? Scampi did you say?

Hendry: I'll mark Ronaldo.

Calderwood: I'll mark Ronaldo.

Dailly: I'll mark Ronaldo.

Boyd: I'll mark Ronaldo.

Collins: How am I looking?

Hendry: Burley, you mark Rivaldo.

Burley: Okay, I've got Ronaldo.

Leighton: For fuck's sake, who was marking Sampaio???

Hendry: I had Ronaldo. It's no' ma fault.

Durie: Did the cameras see it?

Twenty minutes later . . .

Hendry: Shit, here they come again. Crash positions lads.

Leighton: Oh Jesus, humiliation beckons again. Maybe Fergie was right. I'm shite.

Jackson: Oh, there's ma mum in the crowd.

Durie: Bastards the lot of them. I bet they're Catholics.

Dailly: Better get back.

Collins: Feeling like a run. Want to strut these majestic thighs. Looking and feeling great. Plenty of time to score. Oh, here comes the ball. Nice touch, Johnny Boy, you are a God, oh passed him nicely, looking good, need a rest, breaking sweat, I'll gie it to Burley. Beautiful.

Burley: Hi Colin, what are you doing here? Do you want the ball? I think I'm aboot tae get tackled. Shit.

Hendry: I didn't want it ya fanny Craig. Oh shit, here they come again, must hoof it somewhere safe. Where's Jim? Bugger, up the park will do.

Gallacher: Ball coming, must run fast as little legs will carry, then maybe it'll miss me . . . FUCK, WHAT WAS THAT???? A bloody train hit me. Why is everyone hugging me? Am I dead?

Referee: Penalty to Scotland.

Scottish fans: Fuckin' hell.

Hendry: Who wants to take it?

Durie: Errm, ma leg's sore. Old injury.

Gallacher: I've lost a contact lens.

Jackson: Maybe it's no' ma mum.

Collins: Give it tae Johnny Boy, he'll take it. Looking great, I wish Ah had a mirror. Hope the burd is tapin' the game.

McAllister: Now you'll know how it feels, ya wee bastard.

Collins: Let me just place the ball. Millions of burds watching. Cool as a cucumber, Johnners. Right ref, nearly ready. Just fix the hair. Okay, ready to run . . . here we go . . . just one final check, teeth are clean, hair great. Right ladies, watch this . . . and Johnny Boy does it again. Don't touch the fuckin' hair Burley. Hands off my arse Durie. You can get away with that at Rangers, but not here. I can see God on Stars in their Eyes *saying, 'Tonight Matthew, I'm going to be John Collins.'*

McAllister: Fuck.

Craig Brown: Tee hee.

Scottish Fan: Whit? Goal against Brazil? Ya beautyyyyyy. Second round, here we come!!

Leighton: What's happening up there?

Sixteen minutes to go . . .

Hendry: Get rid o' it ya mug!

Lambert: Where?

Hendry: Just hammer it.

Burley: No' tae me ya eejit.

Calderwood: Piss off, Ah had it a minute ago. It's no ma turn, ma kid's watchin'.

Hendry: I said hammer it, not pass it.

Durie: It's too far for me to chase. Go on Kevin.

Gallacher: Come on wee legs, faster. I'm gonna make it. Got it!!! Shit, lost it.

Collins: And his majestic highness steps in to stealthily pass a gorgeous ball to his fellow team mate.

Lambert: I told you, not to me.

Dailly: I don't want it. There's 300 million people watching.

Collins: Is that all? I need a bigger audience. Johnny Boy to the rescue. Who wants a bit of silky skill from the King of all Kings? I think I'll pass to me. Oh yes . . . fantastic, still looking great. Glad I wore that aftershave today . . . What was that?

Gallacher: That was Ronaldo.

Jackson: Can I get a shot on the ball? Ma mum's watching.

Hendry: Somebody tackle Ronaldo.

Calderwood: Okay . . . shit, missed again.

Hendry: Somebody tackle Ronaldo.

Leighton: Who's on the ball now?

Boyd: Dunno.

Leighton: Get markin', I think that's a cross comin' in.

Boyd: I think I'll mark . . . him. He doesn't look dangerous. I should come out of this okay. I can see the newspapers tomorrow, 'Braveheart Boyd a stalwart at the back'.

Leighton: CROSS COMIN' IN!!! I'M GOIN' FOR IT!!!
TOMMY, LOOK OUT . . .

Boyd: Wha'? . . . Oh fuck.

*   *   *

And a sore-sounding one from Wee John of the PTA.
(Not the Parent Teachers Association).

> *I went out for a pint*
> *I got fucking plastered*
> *I went home and beat the wife*
> *She's an English bastard*

In Arnhem, sung to the Dutch:

> *Sing when you're cycling,*
> *You only sing when you're cycling.*

Another from Holland, which is flat to the horizon,
and you think you can see Russia:

> *Wan hill. You've never climbed wan hill . . .*

When Neil Sullivan made his Scotland debut we sang:
You're not English anymore.

Oh, and a classic from Brussels:

5-1 and who gives a fuck?

High hopes on the underground before the game in Brussels with a rendition of:

Scotland's going to Tokyo,
Belgium's going to Butlins,
na na na na, na na na na.

More unwelcome realism:

Bonnie Scotland,
Bonnie Scotland,
We'll support ye up tae four,
We'll support ye up tae four.

From Fringo of the TAMB:
In Brussels, we were taking a time out from the Grand Place and went to a wee corner bar just along the road.

There was the usual procession of local girls walking by and being chatted up by various TA lads. One group of lads managed to stop these two very young ladies and attempted the usual patter. Myself and my mates thought these two might be a touch on the young side so we sang a wee chorus of:

Have you done your homework yet . . .
Have you done your homework yet etc . . .

Also followed by:

Does your mother know you're out?

Response from the other TA guys was the lifting of the kilt to us and the moonlight came out. Top entertainment at the time (you had to be there I suppose).

Tam from the TAMB fires through:
Tallinn, September 2000. Friday night before we left to go on the Battlebus down to Riga. (This is three months after the Euro Champs.) The TA were in Molly's when we spotted the Portugal team in the Old Square (they were in town to play Estonia, the

TA were in town for the craic and punani*). Forty TA all surrounding the Portuguese shaking hands and singing:

> *Thank you very much for beating England,*
> *thank you very much,*
> *thank you very very very much . . .*

It turned out to be the Under-21s and not Figo and Co, but it was still magic.

From Martin of the Balerno TA:

Tune: 'My Old Man's a Dustman'

> *Saint George was an Italian*
> *He's just a Dago chancer*
> *Now he is the Patron Saint*
> *Of all you Morris dancers*
>
> *He's never been to England*
> *He never fought a dragon*
> *If you believe in that auld shite*
> *You deserve a fucking slagging*

---

*TA rhyming slang for female company

FRÈRE JACQUES

There were lots of versions of 'Frère Jacques' drifting in the sunshine in St Etienne and all the cops were called Jean, as in Gendarme.

> *Frère Jacques, Frère Jacques,*
> *Norway drew, Norway drew,*
> *Gaunnae beat Morocco, gaunnae beat Morocco*
> *We're gaun' through, we're gaun through.*

This was later amended to . . .
> *Frère Jacques, Frère Jacques,*
> *Norway drew, Norway drew,*
> *Beaten by Morocco, beaten by Morocco,*
> *We're stuffed noo, we're stuffed noo.*

And a new one for the friendly in France that I made up in ten minutes at the request of Ruary McGregor:

Tune: 'The Marseillaise'

> *We are the famous Tartan A-a-rmy,*
> *And we're here to gub your team.*
> *We also hope to shag your women . . . and men!*
> *Drink your wine and eat your frogs.*
> *Drink your wine and eat your frogs.*

Listen up now, vous Francaisez,
We hope you win the World Cup . . . again!
And you play the way we know you can,
'Cause we're gonny take ten aff ye.

And we're gonny spend our Euros.
Au revoir, le franc Francais.
March on! march on!
We won't be there . . . ya bastard!
But good luck in Japan!

I didn't know that Senegal were going to wanner them, and I bet you didn't either.

And here's the first verse (there are seven) of the real thing, simply the best national anthem ever.

LA MARSEILLAISE

Allons enfants de la patrie
Le jour de gloire est arrivé!
Contre nous de la tyrannie
L'étendard sanglant est levé,
L'étendard sanglant est levé,
Entendez-vous dans les campagnes
Mugir ces féroces soldats?

Ils viennent jusque dans vos bras
Egorger vos fils et vos compagnes!

Refrain
Aux armes, citoyens
Formez vos bataillons.
Marchons, marchons!
Qu'un sang impur
Abreuve nos sillons!

Peter Braughan, film producer, rampant Tim and TA foot soldier, and I, sang the above at the Scotland v Brazil game in France, to approving nods from the French folk there. He also sang it for the Mayor of Bordeaux and got a ticket for that game and two for St Etienne, so it might be worth learning, just in case. Peter is a fecund source of songs and chants. This is one of his from France.

Tune: 'She'll be Coming Round
the Mountain When She Comes'

Ah'm no a Brazilian, Ah'm a Scot,
Ah'm no a Brazilian, Ah'm a Scot,
Ah'm no a Brazilian, Ah'm wan in five million,
Ah'm no a Brazilian, Ah'm a Scot.

Ah'm no a Norwegian, Ah'm a Scot,
Ah'm no a Norwegian, Ah'm a Scot,
Ah'm no a Norwegian. In fact I am Glaswegian,
Ah'm no a Norwegian, Ah'm a Scot.

Ah'm no Morrocan, Ah'm a Scot,
Ah'm no Morrocan, Ah'm a Scot,
Ah'm no Morrocan, ye must be fuckin jokin,
Ah'm no Morrocan, Ah'm a Scot.

Or an alternative 'Marseillaise' from denhaagdavid of the TAMB:

Venez les fils de l'Écosse
que le jour de glorie est ici
mené par des vogts de berti
nous sommes venus à la partie

(Come sons of Scotland
the day of glory is here
led by Berti Vogts
we've come to party)

Nous descendons la route
que nous sommes L'Armée Tartan célèbre
nous n'allons pas a Tokyo
nous n'avons pas voulu aller

(We're coming down the road
we're the famous Tartan Army
we're not going to Tokyo
'cause we didnae want to go)

Ah, optimism . . . not to mention self-delusion. Guess that tune.

We've got the World Cup in our hands,
We've got the World Cup in our hands,
We've got the World Cup in our hands,
We've got the World Cup in our hands.

ALLY'S TARTAN ARMY

We're on the march wi' Ally's Army,
We're gaun tae the Argentine,
And we'll really shake them up,
When we win the World Cup,
'Cos Scotland is the greatest football team.

We're representing Britain,
(Speak for yourself, Andy!)
And we're gaunny do or die,
England canny dae it,
'Cos they didny qualify.

The last two lines are invariably belted out *molto fortissimo* and then everybody kind of loses interest. I was at Hampden for the Argentina leave-taking and I remember bawling out, along with 30,000-odd other hopeless romantics, my other favourite line from the song:

He's our Mohammed Ali, he's Alistair McLeod!

It is still the best official World Cup song for the Scots, combining as it does huge self-belief and over-weening optimism, both very necessary qualities when following Scotland. I had the good fortune to be at a presentation commemorating Argentina by some worthy members of the TAMB. This was to Ally and his wife in the Scottish Football Museum at Hampden, and a tear-producing occasion it was. *Slàinte mhath!* Ally, thanks for the hope, the joy and the laughter.

Wullie Anderson of the TAMB has a slightly more jaundiced (or realistic) view of it:

ALLY'S ARMY

Chorus
We've all been conned by Ally's Army
We went to the Argentine
Oh, we thought we'd be a hit
But we made an arse of it
With the biggest load of crap you've ever seen.

When we got to the Argentine
We thought we were the best
Peru, Iran and Holland
They would fall like all the rest
Then Ally picked his team
And he picked them by their toes
If truth be told the bastard
Couldn't pick his bloody nose.

Chorus

Buchan passed to Hartford
And wee Asa laid it square
And Kenny passed it to the wing
But Johnston wasn't there

Then Ally ran on to the park
And shouted with alarm
'He's in the bloody dug-out shooting
Cocaine up his arm.'

Chorus

We thought the cup was going to be
Presented on a plate
But when the chips were down
We proved to be just second rate
The last few days have surely been
A lesson to us all
The sun doesn't shine out
Ally's arse at all!

Chorus

In France:

> *Scotland's going to Marseille*
> *England's going to Calais*

And on to pastures new . . .

> *Tokyo, Tokyo,*
> *We're the famous Tartan Army*
> *And we're off to Tokyo.*

Followed by the petted lip . . .

> *Tokyo, Tokyo,*
> *We're the famous Tartan Army*
> *And we didny want to go.*

And Tom Small's hopeful, but completely non-prophetic version of Scotland the Brave:

SCOTLAND THE BRAVE 2002

> *I hear the Japs a-calling*
> *And South Korea balling*
> *Loudly and proudly we will march to the East*
> *We'll hae oor kilts a-swinging*

you'll hear oor pipes a-ringing
We'll cheer the finest-ever Scots football team

Chorus
We're off to gain our fame
While England can stay at hame
Our flags and banners they will gloriously wave
Craig Brown will raise our game
And we'll tak the World Cup hame,
We'll cheer the finest-ever Scots football team

Don't be too arty farty
Come an join oor big party
All flags and banners they can gloriously wave
Jump on yer Kawasaki
Join us for a glass of saki
We'll cheer the finest-ever Scots football team

Chorus

We'll march on South Korea
Making friends and drinking beer
We are the best fans that the world has ever seen,
Come join the lads and lassies
Fill up your whisky glasses
We'll cheer the finest-ever Scots football team

Chorus

Scotsmen will come in droves
Welcome the tartan hordes
Were here to party and celebrate the dream.
Our fans are often barmy
Aye, we're the Tartan Army
We'll cheer the finest-ever Scots football team

Chorus

Tom says:

'OK this did not hit *Top o ra Pops* for two very good reasons:

1. We didnae qualify

2. Oor neighbours screwed up the chorus, anyway as they say in the words of that famous song – we have a dream!

Now here's one that really happened, it was the year when the engerlish were coming up here to beat us at the old rugger, good chap. We sort of screwed up their plans big-time. This is not the work of my good self, it was someone on our hardcore TA mailing list:

ODE TO ENGLISH RUGBY

Ye come up here tae paradise, tae beat us at your game,
Aw wind and piss and full o' shit,
Yer aw the bloody same,
Ye caw yersels the champions, the nation's most elite,
Scotland are the champions,
Yuv just been fuckin beat.

A game that wis invented fur English gentlemen,
No Highland Jocks wi' tartan frocks,
well bliddy think again,
A baw that's shapit like an egg, it's jist a stupit farce,
A suppose it maks it easier,
tae ram right up yer arse.

So git back hame an lick yer wounds,
yer a bunch o stupit fools,
It's time fur you tae cheat again, change the fuckin rules,
Rugby, fitba, cricket tae, yer jist a shower o chancers,
Stick tae whit ye dae the best,
you Morris fuckin dancers.

'I converted this one into the Queen's engerlish and sent it down to big Rod*, he was proudly letting every local read it in his TORY club. Aye, you read that right. He makes a point of visiting other clubs around the UK on his travels just to see the look he gets when he arrives at the door.

[*Big Rod is 18-20 stone big, bekilted, and has a beard and hair which he has been growing since the dawn of time. People notice when he walks in, and you tend to remember him. I didn't know he was a Tory.]

'Incidentally, do you know why Morris dancers have clicky sticks and bells?
   So they can piss off blind people as well.'

Balerno TA: a song and a story from Martin Mitchell.

<u>Tune: Eminem's and D12's 'Purple Pills'</u>

We've been to many places
We've painted up our faces
But nothing compares to this Bonnie Scotland
football team

We've climbed the highest mountains
We've swum in many fountains
But nothing compares to this Bonnie Scotland
football team

Tune: 'Sailing', whilst literally doing it opposite the Leaning Tower of Pisa at 5 a.m.

We are crawling, we are crawling, we are crawling across the road.

Tune: 'Scotland the Brave' after the crawling incident

Here comes a Highland gypsy
Head fucked up on Croatian whisky

'It was after San Marino/Zagreb and back home via Pisa and Rome. Day 7: solid drinking and not too many washes sums up how we felt (and looked). One of the boys even had a nightmare that the police in Pisa had rounded us up and thrown us into a fountain for a wash.

You're going home in a Croatian ambulance.

'The background to that is . . .

'One night in Zagreb I approached a Sherpa van waiting at traffic lights with two (I thought) workmen inside and asked for directions to the Hotel Esplanade. I was lost again.

'When I looked in the back I saw an old lady with

a bandage on her head, so made my apologies and went to walk away, but they said: 'No, no. It's OK.' One of them got out with a map to show me directions to the hotel, or so I thought.

'He told me to get in, so there I was sat between two ambulance drivers in my kilt. "Five minutes, OK, first we take the grandmother to the hospital." How could I argue with that? They dropped her off and then dropped me back at the hotel.'

And from his mate Ian Learmonth:

'As it was just after the court case . . .
'During Wembley '99 we were singing Gary Glitter songs all day, to the bemusement of the England supporters, until we followed it up with:

> *Gary Glitter's English,*
> *Gary Glitter's English,*
> *na na na na.'*

If you are not yet a Tamber, it is time you were. You are missing brilliant stuff like this. And if you don't get the references, tough.

From McEminem:

RUARY
<u>Tune: 'Stan'</u>

My tea's gone cold I'm wondering why I went on the TAMB at all,
    'Cos AOB is rubbish and I own Gener-al, and even though I'm hard, and think I'm it, Got Mirza's picture on my wall, it reminds me that he's still the man, he's still the man.

Dear Mirza, I PM'd you but you still ain't talkin', I left my cell, my pager and the Heb Bar's number at the bottom, I started two threads for you back in autumn, you must not of seen them, there probably was a problem in Sarajevo or something, sometimes I give the thread a stupid title when I start them, but anyways, fuck it, what's been up man how's Bosnia, my new wife's pregnant too, I'm out to prove I'm not gay, if I have a daughter guess what I'm going to call her, I'm going to name her Didier, I read the posts by Trolls slagging you, I'm sorry, I had a friend who won't come on the board because of some Troll that made fun of him, I know you hear this on the TAMB every day, but I'm your biggest fan, I've even got the underground site that you did with Dianne, I've got a room full of stuff from the Sunshine Appeal man, I liked the designs you posted on the board for the new Scotland tops too, those strips were smart, anyways I hope you get this man, PM me back, just a chat, truly yours your biggest fan Ruary, king of the TAMB.

My tea's gone cold I'm wondering why I went on the TAMB at all, 'Cos AOB is rubbish and I own Gener-al, and even though I'm hard, and think I'm it, Got Mirza's picture on my wall it reminds me that he's still the man, he's still the man.

Dear Mirza, you still haven't PM'd or wrote, I hope you have a chance, I ain't mad I just think it's fucked up you don't answer the king of the TAMB, if you didn't want to talk to me outside Pandora's you didn't have to but you could have signed a Glengarry for Allan, that's the guy who types in blocked capitals man, he's only got about six posts though, we waited on Victoria road for you for four hours and you just said no, that's pretty shitty man, you're like his fuckin' idol, he wants to be just like you man, he wants to be a moderator more than I do, I ain't that mad though, I just don't like people knowing more about the TAMB than I do, remember when we met in the Iron Horse you said if I texted you, you would text back, see I'm just like you in a way, I never had a life either, I would always challenge my mum to see who could get the most posts on the TAMB and beat her, I can relate to what you're saying on the TAMB, so when I have a shitty day I can drift away when I turn the pc on, 'cos I don't really have anything else, so the TAMB helps when I'm depressed, I've even got a tattoo with AlbaGuBrath across the chest, sometimes I turn my pc off, but then I have to abort, the pain is a sudden rush for me with out the TAMB technical support, see everything you post is good and I respect you 'cos you tell it, my BT bill's huge 'cos I'm on the internet 24/7, other Tambers don't know you like I know you Mirza, no one knows what goes wrong, they don't know what it was like for us logging-on, you got to PM me man I'll be the biggest Tamber you'll ever lose sincerely yours, Ruary, ps we should be co-administrators too.

My tea's gone cold I'm wondering why I went on the TAMB at all, 'Cos AOB is rubbish and I own Gener-al, and even though I'm hard, and think I'm it, Got Mirza's picture on my wall it reminds me that he's still the man, he's still the man.

Dear Mr Owner of the TAMB, this'll be the last message I ever send your ass, its been six months and still no word, I don't deserve this, I know you saw my last two threads I posted them in Scottish Fitba Lassies and Any Other Business, so this is the web-cam I'm sending you, I hope you see it. I'm in the Battlebus right now I'm doing ninety in the deprived western fringes, hey McMirza, I've drunk a fifth of pear cider dare me to drive, you know the song by the Proclaimers '500 miles' by those two speccy twins who would have walked anywhere but didn't, and McTeagle saw it all and thought the song was about him, that's kind of how this is, you could of rescued me from DoricDuncan, now it's too late I've done 3000 posts now I'm drowsy and all I wanted was a lousy message or asked if I was ok, I hope you know I've put all of the Sunshine Appeal items up for sale on TAMB-bay, I loved you Mirza we could have been administrators together, think about it, you've ruined it now I hope you can't enjoy games and you dream about it, and when you dream I hope you can't post and you scream about it, I hope your avatar eats at you and you can't start topics without me, see Mirza, shut up bitch I'm trying to talk, hey Mirza, that's Lamia and Thermopoof screaming in the trunk, but I didn't slit their throats I just cut off their internet connection because if they go without the TAMB for more than five minutes they'll suffer more and then they'll cry too, well gotta go I'm almost at the Kingston bridge now, oh shit I forgot how am I meant to send this shit out.

My tea's gone cold I'm wondering why I went on the TAMB at all, 'Cos AOB is rubbish and I own Gener-al, and even though I'm hard, and think I'm it, Got Mirza's picture on my wall, it reminds me that he's still the man, he's still the man.

Dear Ruary, I meant to PM you sooner but I just been busy, you said your wife almost has 1000 posts now, how far along is she, look I'm really flattered that you went to the Iron Horse and not the Horseshoe, here's an autograph for Allan I signed it on a sgian dubh, *I'm sorry I didn't see you in Pandora's, don't think I'm gay, I must have been hanging out with Andy Gray, and what's this shit you said about how you like to turn off your pc too, I say that shit just clowning is all c'mon how fucked up is you, you've got some issues Ruary and maybe someone can help you, if you want I can put you in touch with m1 or m2, and what's this shit about us being co-administrators, that's like the shit that makes me think you're a traitor, I really think you and the TAMB need each other or maybe you just have to post a lot better, I hope you get to read this message, I just hope it reaches you in time, before you turn off your pc, I think you'll be doing just fine if you relax a little, I'm glad you're a Tamber, but Ruary why are you so sad, try to understand that I do want you to continue with your TAMB literature, I just don't like your crazy shit like your bent signature, I seen this one thread on the TAMB a couple of weeks ago that made me sick, some guy started a stupid thread that got about a million replies it was quite a while ago so I can't remember why, and now on the board it's probably pretty low, come to think of it the title was 'In the glory of God I go'.*

Damn.

WE LOVE YOU SCOTLAND

We love you Scotland, we do,
We love you Scotland, we do,
We love you Scotland, we do,
Oh Scotland we love you.

AWAY IN A MANGER

Away in a manger
No crib for a bed
The little Lord Jesus
Lay down and he said . . .

Oooooooh Scotland
(nanananana)
Scotland
I'd walk a million miles
For one of your goals
Oh Scotland.

From Campbell Anderson – this is a favourite of the Campbeltown Tartan Army and was first sung in the pub and on the bus prior to the Latvia match. It goes to the tune of 'D.I.S.C.O.'

S.C.O.T.S.

We are S.C.O.T.S
We are S.C.O.T.S
We are S.C.O.T.S
We are S.C.O.T.S
We are S. Some supporters
We are C. Completely barmy
We are O. On the bevvy
We're the T. Tartan Army
We are So, oh, oh
We are S.C.O.T.S etc, etc, etc . . .

WHERE'S YIR FAITHER, REFEREE?

Where's yir Faither,
Where's yir Faither,
Where's yir Faither, Referee?
Ye huvny got one,
Ye huvny got one,
You're a bastard, referee.

Some advice on chariots for our charioteering cousins:

You can stick your fucking chariots up your arse.
You can stick your fucking chariots up your arse.
You can stick your fucking chariots,
Stick your fucking chariots.
Stick your fucking chariots up your arse.

Ditties from Minsk:

We're not 30 we're section 29
We drink vodka and bottles of wine
Meths and beer and turpentine
We're section 29

There's a moose loose aboot Belaroos!

Note: a moose is a wee rodent that likes living behind skirting boards, etc – not a great big hairy thing the size of a horse with pointy bits coming out of its head – unless you want it to be.

FUCK ALL

<u>to be sung to the tune of Oasis chart-topper</u>
<u>'Wonderwall'</u>

And after all, we're gonny win fuck all . . .

And some old and all-time favourites:

BONNIE DUNDEE

To the Lords of convention 'twas Claverhouse spoke,
Ere the King's crown go down there are crowns
to be broke,
So each cavalier that loves honour and me
Let him follow the bonnets o' bonnie Dundee.

Chorus
Come fill up my cup, come fill up my can,
Come saddle my horses and call up my men,
Unhook the West Port and let us gae free
For it's up with the bonnets o' Bonnie Dundee.

Dundee he is mounted, he rides up the street,
The bells they ring backward, the drums they are beat,
But the provost (douce man) said: 'Just e'en let it be,
For the toun is weel rid o' that deil o' Dundee!'

Chorus

There are hills beyond Pentland, and lands beyond Forth
Be there lords in the south, there are chiefs in the north
There are brave Duinnewassals three thousand times three
Will cry: 'Hey for the bonnets o' Bonnie Dundee.'

Chorus

Then awa to the hills, to the lea, to the rocks,
Ere I own a usurper, I'll couch with the fox;
And tremble, false Whigs, in the midst of your glee
Ye hae no seen the last of o' my bonnets and me.

Chorus

TWA RECRUITIN' SERGEANTS

Twa recruitin' sergeants cam fae the Black Watch,
To markets and fairs some recruits for to catch,
An' a' that they listed was for forty an' twa,
So list my bonnie laddie an' come awa.

Chorus
It is over the mountains and over the main,
Through Gibraltar to France and Spain,
Get a feather tae your bonnet and a kilt abune your knee,

An' list bonnie laddie an' come awa wi' me.

Oh laddie, ye dinna ken the danger that ye're in,
If your horses wis to fleg an' your ousen wis to rin,
This greedy auld fairmer winna pey your fee,
So list bonnie laddie an' come awa wi' me.

Chorus

It is intae the barn an' oot o' the byre,
This auld fairmer thinks ye'll never tire,
For it's a slavery job of low degree,
So list bonnie laddie an' come awa wi' me.

Chorus

Wi' your tatty poorins an' your meal an' kail,
Your soor sowen soorins an' your ill-brewed ale,
Wi' your buttermilk and whey an' your breid fired raw,
So list bonnie laddie an' come come awa.

Chorus

Oh, laddie if ye've got a sweetheart an' bairn,
Ye'll easily get rid o' that ill-spun yarn,
Twa rattles o' the drum an' that'll pey it a',
So list bonnie laddie an' come awa.

LOCH LOMOND

By yon bonnie banks and by yon bonnie braes,
Where the sun shines bright on Loch Lomond,
Where me and my true love were ever wont to gae,
On the bonnie, bonnie banks o' Loch Lomond.

Chorus
For you'll take the high road and I'll take the low road,
And I'll be in Scotland afore ye,
Where me and my true love will never meet again,
By the bonnie, bonnie banks of Loch Lomond.

'Twas there we parted in yon shady glen,
On the steep, steep side of Ben Lomond,
Where in purple hue the Hieland hills we view,
An' the moon comin' out in the gloamin'.

Chorus

The wee birdies sing and the wild flowers spring,
And in sunshine the waters are sleeping,
But the broken heart it knows no second spring,
Tho' the waefu' may cease frae their greetin'.

Chorus

I WILL GO

Chorus
I will go, I will go,
When the fighting is over,
To the land o' McLeod,
That I left to be a soldier,
I will go, I will go.

When the King's son came along,
He called us a' together,
Saying 'Brave Highland men,
Will you fight for my father?'

Chorus

I've a buckle on my belt,
A sword in my scabbard,
A red coat on my back,
And a shilling in my pocket.

Chorus

When they put us all on board,
The lassies were singing,
But the tears came tae their eyes,
When the bells started ringing.

Chorus

When we landed on the shore,
And we saw the foreign heather,
We knew that some would fall,
And would stay there for ever.

Chorus

When we got back to the glen,
The winter was turning,
Our goods lay in the snow,
And our houses were burning.

Chorus

You have to ask yourself at some point if wee Cliff Hanley was at the wind-up with the one on the next page. Not a lot of people know the words, though at one point the SFA, in their far from infinite wisdom, touted this as our official national anthem. The ultimate in absurdity was achieved in Iceland, when our very gracious hosts wheeled on a grand piano and a forty-strong choir, which sang every word of every verse, with the troops on the terraces going na na na na na na na with red faces. I was one of them and I learned the song the next day, but I rarely sing it. There is, though, a kind of jumpy-up-and-down pogo dance that goes with it that is good fun to take part in while going na na na etc.

SCOTLAND THE BRAVE

Hark where the night is falling
Hark hear the pipes a calling
Loudly and proudly calling down through the glen
There where the hills are sleeping
Now feel the blood a-leaping
High as the spirits of the old Highland men

Towering in gallant fame
Scotland my mountain hame
High may your proud standards gloriously wave
Land of my high endeavor
Land of the shining river
Land of my heart forever, Scotland the Brave

High in the misty mountains
Out by the purple highlands
Brave are the hearts that beat beneath Scottish skies
Wild are the winds to meet you
Staunch are the friends that greet you
Kind as the love that shines from fair maidens' eyes

And another version from Thermopylae:

We are the Tartan Army
Don't be feart 'cos we'll nae harm ye
We've a million songs tae charm ye
Berti's Boys
We are the Tartan Army
Don't be feart 'cos we'll nae harm ye
We've a million songs tae charm ye
Berti's Boys

Oslo first is where we'll be
Then we're aff tae Germany
Berti Vogts is going home and we know we'll score
two or three
For we are the Tartan Army
Don't be feart 'cos we'll nae harm ye
We've a million songs tae charm ye
Berti's Boys

WILD MOUNTAIN THYME

O the summer time is come
And the trees are sweetly blooming
And the wild mountain thyme grows
Around the blooming heather
Will ye go, lassie, go?

Chorus
And we'll all go together
To pluck wild mountain thyme
All around the blooming heather
Will ye go, lassie, go?

I will build my love a bower
Near yon pure crystal fountain
And on it I will bigg
All the flooers o' the mountain
Will ye go, lassie, go?

Chorus

If my true love she were gone
I would surely find another
Where wild mountain thyme
Grows around the blooming heather
Will ye go, lassie, go?

Chorus

Repeat verse 1 and chorus

Dougie McLean's brand-new classic:

CALEDONIA

I don't know, if you can see
The changes that have come over me.
These last few days I've been afraid
that I might drift away.
I've been telling old stories, singing songs,
That make me think about where I come from.
That's the reason why I seem so far away today.

Chorus
Let me tell you that I love you,
And I think about you all the time.
Caledonia, you're calling me and now I'm going home.
If I should become a stranger,
You know that it would make me more than sad.
Caledonia's been everything I've ever had.

I have moved and I've kept on moving,
Proved the points that I needed proving.
Lost the friends that I needed losing,
Found others on the way.

I have kissed the ladies and left them crying,
Stolen dreams, yes, there's no denying.
I have travelled hard, sometimes with conscience flying,
Somewhere with the wind.

Chorus

Now I'm sitting here before the fire,
The empty room, the forest choir.
The flames that couldn't get any higher,
They've withered now they've gone.

But I'm steady thinking, my way is clear,
And I know what I will do tomorrow.
When the hands have shaken and the kisses flowed,
Then I will disappear.

Chorus, and once more with feeling

For my money, the above is the best Scottish nostalgia

song ever written. This is another:

THE FLOO'ERS O' THE FOREST

I've heard them lilting at our yowe-milking,
Lasses a' liltin' before the dawn o' day;
But now they are moaning on ilka green loaning,
The Floo'ers o' the Forest are a' wede away.

At buchts, in the morning, nae blythe lads are scorning,
The lasses are lonely and dowie and wae;
Nae daffin, nae gabbin', but sighing and sabbing,
Ilk ane lifts her leglen and hies her away.
In hairst, at the shearing, nae youths now are jeering,
The bandsters are lyart and runkled and grey:
At fair, or at preaching, nae wooing, nae fleeching,
The Floo'ers o' the Forest are a' wede away.

At e'en in the gloaming, nae swankies are roaming
'Bout stacks wi' the lasses at bogle to play;
But ilk ane sits drearie, lamenting her dearie,
The Floo'ers o' the Forest are a' wede away.

Dule and wae for the order sent our lads to the Border!
The English, for ance, by guile wan the day;
The Floo'ers o' the Forest, that foucht aye the foremost,
The prime o' our land are cauld in the clay.

We'll hear nae mair lilting at the yowe-milking,
Women and bairns are heartless and wae;
Sighing and moaning on ilka green loaning,
The Floo'ers o' the Forest are a' wede away.

One for the Jubilee. It is more than twenty-five years since 1977, when we did our Wembley rehab. I owe Gaberlunzie an apology for this, as in the first edition they were not credited with copyright of the song. In my own defence might I say that I thought that it had been written by Tom Small, the Battlebus Commander, as he sings it a lot, mostly through his tartan megaphone. Anyhow, they were most gracious about it, and here it is again, credited properly this time to © GABERLUNZIE MUSIC 1979. It is a cracking song.

HAPPY HOOLIGANS O' WEMBLEY

Oh, I wear a tartan bunnet and a scarf around my throat
And I can sing the Flower of Scotland every single note
For we're gan doon tae London toun
Tae paralyse the undergroond
And we're just the happy hooligans of Wembley.

Chorus
So it's o'er the border if ye dare

And doon tae London for a tear
We're just the happy hooligans of Wembley.
When Scotland's playing England, oh it really fills
my heart
Wi' a' the flags and banners, aye we surely look the part
But win or lose it's aw the same
We didny come tae see the game
We're just the happy hooligans o' Wembley.

Chorus

Oh there's forty in my party, aye and that's including me
We havnae a' got tickets, in fact we've only three
And three will win the lucky draw
The rest'll be climbing o'er the wa'
We're just the happy hooligans o' Wembley.

Chorus

We're going to see how many pints that we can
sink away
We're going to drink auld London dry, we'll drink it
dry today
And before we've even seen a baw
We'll piss it up against the wa'
We're just the happy hooligans o' Wembley.

Chorus

And now the fun is over and we've finished aw the beer
We couldnae go back tae Scotland withoot a souvenir
So maybe for a wee bit lark
We'll dig up half o' Wembley park
We're just the happy hooligans o' Wembley.

Chorus

Now we're back in Scotland after all the deeds are done
We dinnae really give a damn if Scotland lost or won
For we met the English, had our fun,
Reminded them o' Bannockburn.
We're just the happy hooligans of Wembley.

Chorus

Did I mention that the above song should be credited to © GABERLUNZIE MUSIC 1979? Thanks to Gordon Menzies and the rest of the group for letting me off lightly.

Here is another verse that really was written by Tom Small:

We hope to go Portugal, to have three weeks of fun,

We'll hae a wee swally, we'll party in the sun,
And if we're knocked out, and our trip cut short,
Well, fuck it we'll drink all their port, cos we're etc . . .

And now we're off to Dortmund, to wave our banner high,
We'll have a beer festival, we'll drink the place dry,
When we top the group, and we're gaun through,
I'll nae be sober for a week or two, cos we're the HH etc.

ONE TEAM IN TALLINN

One team in Tallinn
There's only one team in Tallinn
One team in Tallinn
There's only one team in Tallinn

The game that never was, sung when Estonia didn't appear for the game.

SCOTLAND IN ESTONIA (POEM)

In Tallinn the Old Town, by Raekoja Plats Square
The skirl of the pipes could be heard in the air
At Kaddriorg Park, the justice was cruel

FIFA decided to change all their rules
The meeting was final with a decision agreed
Chaired by Johansson, group rivals, a Swede
How can they treat great fans in this way
We've seen all their placards that proclaim fair play!
Through Denmark and Finland and Baltic seaways
The loyal Tartan Army had travelled for days
One week and more, in Estonia they stayed
In hotels and bars, they boosted the trade
Scotland in Estonia, what a strange game
Three seconds of glory and fame
We travel the world, to see football played
With FIFA in charge, the price that we paid.

© *Stuart Logan, 1996.*

Sent to FIFA by fax in protest about the decision that Scotland should have to replay against Estonia after the Estonians failed to turn up for the original match.

I *learned* this pish, now it's your turn. Thus is the cycle of abuse perpetuated.

YABBA DABBA DOO

Ya-ba-dabba-doo
We support the boys in blue

And it's easy, easy
Ya-ba-dabba-doo
We are gonna follow you
And it's easy, easy

Ya-ba-dabba-day
We'll be with you all the way
Singing easy, easy

Ring-a-ding-a-ding
There goes Willie on the wing
And it's easy, easy
Ring-a-ding-a-ding
Knock it over for the king
And it's easy, easy

Ring-a-ding-a-dong
Now we know we can't go wrong
And it's easy, easy

Come on

Now we're really gonna roll
Gotta get another goal
Oh! Oh! Oh! Come on
Just another one to win
Stick it in! Stick it in!

Stick it in!

Eeny-meeny-mo
Get the ball and have a go
And it's easy, easy
Eeny-meeny-mo
We'll let everybody know
That it's easy, easy
Eeny-meeny-my
Now we're really flying high
And it's easy, easy

I have sung this, in foreign climes, wi' a few o' my cronies, with tears in my eyes. And I'm originally from Motherwell.

I BELONG TO GLASGOW

I've been wi' a few o' my cronies,
One or two pals o' my ain;
We went in a hotel,
We did very well,
Aye, and then we came out once again.

And then we went into anither,
That is the reason I'm fou;
We had six deoch-an-doruses, sang a few choruses,
Just listen, I'll sing it to you:

Chorus
I belong to Glasgow,
Dear old Glasgow town;
But there's something the matter wi' Glasgow,
For it's goin' round and round.
I'm only a common old working chap,
As anyone here can see,
But when I get a couple o' drinks on a Saturday,
Glasgow belongs to me!

There's nothing in being teetotal,
And saving a shilling or two;
If your money you spend,
You've nothing to lend,
Isn't that all the better for you;
There's nae harm in taking a drappie,
It ends all your trouble and strife;
And it gives ye the feeling that when you land home,
Well, you don't care a hang for your wife!

Chorus

Just before the last World Cup, there was the predictable debate about whether the Scottish support should get behind the English team. These are some ditties expressing a view on the subject – mine, in point of fact – and I wrote some of them so that I could sing them on Edwina Currie's radio programme. The TAMB contributed the rest. It all happened over one evening before I went on the programme and I can't remember who did what.

Tune: 'Ally's Tartan Army'

We're the famous Tartan Army,
We're not going to Japan,
We saw the price of beer,
And thought it was too dear,
So instead we're drinking Tennents from a can.
We're in the pub the Tartan Argie,
Watching the World Cup on TV,
We're keeping very quiet,
Watching England fans riot,
'Coz they just got stuffed 11-3.

We will be supporting Argentina,
'Cause we've always liked Eva Perón,
We will cheer and eff and blind,

As the Argies bang them in,
And England's misery goes on and on.

We greatly admire Ingmar Bergman,
'Cause Sweden is a country that we like,
And as Larsson scores the goals,
We'll be eating sausage rolls,
And England will be put upon their bike.

The wee Nigerian did the bouncy,
When he scored against the Scots,
Imagine what he'll do,
When he rams in number two,
And gives the rotten English team the trots.

We're on the piss, the Tartan Army,
We're lying flat upon oor backs,
But we'll raise a great big cheer,
an' drink another pint o' beer,
When the Argies knock out the Sassenachs.

I cannae bend the ball like Beckham,
I cannae score like Michael O,
But I dinnae gie a fuck,
Because I know it don't need luck,
For Argentina to beat England four zero.

We're on the couch, the Tartan Army,
We've got everything that we'll be needin',
We've got lager, beer and rum,
And we're gonny have some fun,
Watchin' England getting humped again fae Sweden.

We're on the piss the Tartan Army,
We're all totally Magooed*,
An' we'll huv a laugh at Sven,
When wee Henrik knocks in ten,
An' sticks the Larsson licker somewhere rude.

*There is a Tartan Army foot soldier called Magoo.
He is the one in the green piper's jacket and orange
kilt and his entire back is a tattoo of Scotland. When
you meet him, anywhere in the world, morning, noon
or night, he is always totally, utterly and completely
steaming. Thus: 'Let's go and get Magooed,' or: 'Christ,
was I Magooed last night.'
Magoo was hospitalised for four days after he was
attacked by five English thugs for the crime of jumping
up when he thought that Denmark had scored against
England. There is not an ounce of harm or nastiness
in the man. Don't believe it when you read that the

English fans have reformed. Some of us would like to meet these brave men, if they care to come forward, for a spot of re-education.

We're the famous Tartan Argies
And we're playing in Sapporo
And we'll really shut them up
When we beat England in the cup
With a hat trick from Hernen MacCrespo

We didny want to go to Tokyo
'Cause England and us are on the outs
So we'll stay at home instead, eating lots of jam and bread
And enjoy ourselves while cheering on the Krauts

And a longer version:

We've got Crespo, Gonzalez and Batistuta too
Aimar and Ortega all wearing white and blue
Saviola, Lopez and Claudio Cannigia
Juan Sebastian Veron, he's our Davie Weir

Chorus
We are Henrik Larsson's Sweden
We've got a really good team
And we'll really make some noise

When we beat Sven-Goran's boys
And start to sing 'I Have a Dream'

Scotland didnae make it, they didnae qualify
But they'll be backing anyone to take out Beckham's boys
England will go home early, the English press will moan
'We didnae win it because of Beck's broken bone'

Chorus

We are Kanu's super-eagles
We're off to the Far East
We'll be doing somersaults, backflips and the rest
When we send the English team back to the West

Chorus

Our manager was Craigie Brown
He shagged about the town
But now he's gone and given up
Before the World Cup
The new man's Berti Vogts
He's lifted all our hopes
His nickname is Der Terrier
And he's our number one

Heard a guy singing this in Belgium. He sent me the words but I've lost his name. Thank you, guy in MacGregor tartan with a paint brush for a sporran. He sang all of this from memory. Personally, I think he should change his restaurant.

INDIAN CURRY RHAPSODY

Naan, I just killed a man,
Poppadom against his head,
Had lime pickle now he's dead.
Naan, dinner's just begun,
But now I'm gonna crap it all away.
Naan, ooh ooh ooh,
Didn't mean to make you cry,
Ain't seen nothing yet, just wait to see the loo tomorrow,
Curry on, curry on,
'Cause nothing really madras,
Too late my dinner's going,
Send shivers down my spine,
Rectum aching all the time,
Goodbye onion bhajis, I've got to go,
Gotta leave you all behind and use the loo,
Naan, ooh ooh ooh,
The dopiazi is so mild,
Sometimes wish we'd never come here at all.
I see a little chicken tikka on the side,

Rogan josh, rogan josh, pass the chutney made of mango,
Vindaloo does nicely,
Very very spicy,
Birriani (birriani),
Birriani (birriani),
Birriani and a naan,
A vindaloo loo loo loo,
I've eaten balti, somebody help me,
He's eaten balti, get him to a lavatory,
Stand you well back,
'Cause the loo is quarantined,
Here it comes,
There it goes,
Technicoloured naan,
I chunder,
No,
It's coming up again,
No no no no no no no,
On my knees, I'm on my knees,
On his knees, he's on his knees,
This vindaloo,
It's about to wreck my guts,
Poor me, poor me, poor me-ee-ee.

So you think you can chunder and feel alright,
So you try to eat curry and drink beer all night,
Oh maybe, but now you puke like a baby,

Just had to come out,
It just had to come right out in here.

Findlay Hickey wrote this. I didn't credit it in the first edition of this book because I didn't know. I still owe him a beer. Also, Findlay's brother Maurice (aka Maurice fae Forres) wrote some of the France '98 ones.

DON'T LET'S BE BEASTLY TO THE ENGLISH

Don't let's be beastly to the English,
When the Cup is ultimately won.
It was just those nasty tabloids
That encouraged them to fight,
And all their pomp and circumstance
Is far worse than its bite.
Let's be meek to them
And turn the other cheek to them
And try to bring out their latent sense of fun.
Let's give them what they think they're due
And say we wish they'd battled through,
But don't let's be beastly to the scum.
We must be kind, and with an open mind,
We must endeavour to play the game,

To let the English know that when the fighting's over,
They were not the ones who were to blame.
We must be sweet and tactful and discreet,
And when they've suffered defeat,
We mustn't let them feel upset,
Or ever get the feeling that we're cross with them or
hate them,
Our future policy must be to never bait them.

Don't let's be beastly to the English,
For Schadenfreude it really isn't done,
Let us treat them very kindly
As we would a valued friend,
And strong supportive shoulders to the vanquished we
must lend.
Let's be sweet to them and day by day repeat to them
That hooliganism simply isn't done.
Let's help the filthy clowns again
To smash up foreign towns again,
But don't let's be beastly to the scum.
We must be just and win their love and trust
And in addition we must be wise,
And ask the smashed-up towns to help us to
applaud them,
That would be a wonderful surprise!
For many years, they've been in floods of tears,
Because the poor little dears

Have been so wronged and only longed
To cheat the world, deplete the world and beat the world
to blazes,
This is the moment when we ought to sing their praises.

Don't let's be beastly to the English,
For you can't deprive a bully of his fun.
Though they were a little naughty in the city of
Marseilles,
It would have been unkind to keep the rascals from
their play.
Let's be free with them and give up the BBC to them,
We mustn't prevent them basking in the sun.
Let's soften their defeat again,
And let them have a bleat again,
But don't let's be beastly to the scum.

Don't let's be beastly to the English,
When another sporting season has begun.
We must send them our best wishes,
Give them all the cheer they need,
For an English fan's intentions can be always guaranteed.
Let's accede to them and all our sport concede to them,
They're better than us at honest manly fun.
Let's let them feel as swell again,
And bore us all to hell again,
But don't let's be beastly to the scum.

This next is from the song sheet on the bus to the ladies' game against Austria at Livingston. Not a few of us have taken up the cause of the women and the home gates are now over a thousand and growing rapidly, including a male TA contingent in the full fig. It is like the old days (said the old guy nostalgically), when everybody knew everyone else, and it is simply terrific.

Tune: 'Land of Hope and Glory'

We hate the Von Trapp family
And Kurt Waldheim too
We didn't like the Anschluss
And Austria . . . we don't like you!

This one was, hand up to God, written by an Austrian friend of mine.

Tune: 'Edelweiss'

Austria, Austria
Gonny go and get lost-ia
We will winnnnnnn

You will lose . . .
That's for what ye did to the Jews

The ladies beat Austria and this, which I wrote for *The Herald*, details the consequences:

'It all seemed so simple at the time. I've been on dozens of buses this season. How difficult could it be to run one? We were sitting in the Tap Shop bar in West Calder just after the game against Austria, when Scotland's female footballers totally gubbed them 5-0, taking us to within three points of Belgium, who top the section with fifteen points from six games, with a goal difference of plus four. That win meant we only needed to beat Wales to win the section, because we had scored four against Belgium in our home game and now have a goal difference of plus thirteen. Wales have no points in the section and they don't even want to think about their goal difference. Topping the section means we qualify for the World Cup play-offs.

'My mouth lives a wild and free life of its own, sometimes, and I heard it saying: "We could go to Wales to see them do it." Wullie Anderson and his wife Gill were right behind me and the idea blossomed and spread its petals faster than a desert cactus. "Wales. Wales! Wales?" The word ricocheted around the Tap Shop like a bagatelle ball on speed.

'Supporting the women is a new thing for the Tartan Army. There were around 60 of the fully tartaned and kilted-up diehards at the Belgian game and, as the word spread on the Tartan Army Message Board that here we had a team which won, about 150 foot soldiers turned up for the Austrian game and we stood and sang and cheered our hearts out for the whole time. We even made up songs. And did we make up songs for the bus to Wales? Does rain fall downwards? Here's a verse from one of Bridie Boy's efforts:

We came on a bus on a long, long drive,
We're here to see Scotland win Group Five,
We wear the kilts and we jump and jive,
Taffy, whaur's yer boozers?

'Dianne Small even printed a song sheet for us and all of the hassles I had had busrunning-wise vanished as we raised our voices. After a totally brilliant evening in the Merthyr Tydfil FC social club, at whose ground the game was played, and a national Scotland/Wales song-singing competition outside after it shut, we were up bright and early the day of the game.

'Aye right. We were back at the social club next day, but not early. And not bright. The game itself was scrappy early on. A chant of *"Brazil, it's just like watching Brazil"*, segued into *"Miss World, it's just like watching*

Miss World", in an attempt to spur Scotland on. The first half was a pretty dispiriting affair, with the gloom relieved only by Wales missing a penalty in the thirtieth minute, when Ceryl Jones hit the left-hand post and the ball bounced into the welcoming arms of Gemma Fay, for me the woman of the match. Scotland started the second half as though manager Vera Pauw had personally poked a flea into every single ear. In twelve minutes Donna James looked up, saw the Welsh keeper off her line and curled a beauty all of forty yards into the net. (Ronaldinho must have seen a video of this and copied it against England.) Scotland then came more into the game and started to dominate and, if Donna had scored the sitter she missed in twenty minutes, it would have been all over. As you know, there is a law of Scottish women's football which says that the game isn't over till Julie Fleeting scores and, with five minutes to go, the inevitable happened and Julie rolled it through a forest of legs into the keeper's left-hand corner and the game was over.

Brilliant weekend, top of the league, only running the bus to Prague or maybe the Ukraine to worry about. Let the good times, and the buses, roll.'

Then there was this slightly more unofficial report for the TAMB posters and their avatars, some of which we took with us. For the uninitiated, an avatar is the wee cartoon symbol which you can choose to be beside your name on a message board. There are thousands available and nearly everyone on the TAMB has a different one. Dianne made laminates of the avatars of people who gave us a donation and we took one each and carried them everywhere, texting and phoning their owners to let them know what they were getting up to.

Blackie the Busrunner reporting here.
Shame on you TAMB tattletales re the delicate blossoming of a fragile romance between that blushing rose of maidenly innocence, Dianne, and that flower of Scottish chivalry, Sacks. What happens on the bus stays on the bus and I promise not to mention the highly unofficial marriage which took place on it. Lionheart, the TA trip virgin, deflowered himself in spectacular fashion and the only totey rap on the knuckles was for The Claw and some tiny misdemeanours like trying to drive the bus away and some dangerous work with curtains in the Social Club. Kev was badly overserved on the way down and spent a fair amount of time contemplating his crotch, but then who among us has not at some time had that Buddhist-on-beta-blockers feeling, that realisation that you have discovered a Grand Canyon of the

mind and are falling, screaming soundlessly, through it for ever? Not me, of course, I just have a good imagination.

We do have a new dance, which the Vice Captain and Credit Card can be contacted about if you wish to learn the motions (a snip at £50 an hour) and, thanks to Wullie and Gill, a complete knowledge of the most totally awful and crap Scottish music in the history of the entire peoples of Scotland plus 10 billion years. And we are the balloon light-sabre killer-drillers of the known universe.

Dianne and the Battlebus Commander's songsheet has got some of the best ever, including 'We're on the March with Vera's Army'. Contact her for copies, all profits to the Sunshine Appeal.

Twenty-two of Scotia's finest on the bus plus twelve avatars. Total avatar kitty £120 and totally brilliant. It went on, in order of dispensation, and size does matter here: BOOZE, accommodation for the couple of totally skint folk that came along, the driver and a well-deserved tenner for the bloke who ran the disco at Merthyr Tydfil FC social club on Saturday night. It would be fair to say that a good time was had by all, especially the one of us who got off with the lady with the build of a second-row forward, and that the singing was special.

Read Monday's *Herald* for a match report. Did we

get a welcome from the women when they saw the flags and banners? Does Dolly Parton sleep on her back? Did we get hugs, kisses and not a few tears from them after the game? Darn tootin' we did. Did Marit dispense goodies? Did Vera seem marriage-threateningly attractive? (Or was that just me?) Did we buy out the club shop and return with bags full of eminently desirable (and saleable: Sunshine Fund) souvenirs? Did Moira turn out to be a *chanteuse nonpareil*? That's 'yes' times four.

And there is more, so much more.

To those of you who were there, 'Yo!' We know how we feel, we band of brothers and sisters. To those of you who were not, 'Milk, lemonade, chocolate!' Youse missed yourselves something rotten.

Cheers,

Ian

PS Give me a break on Prague for a few days.

Here's JimFaeKdy's (posted by JimFaeKdy on 4:42 p.m. on 20 May 2002):
Blackie's report sums the trip up really.

Best Darts Player: Dianne . . . she beat maself, Bridie Boy and Sacks at killer darts . . . not a great deal of competition for her.

Best Dancer: That goes to Bridie Boy . . . you can

dae things wi' yer legs a didn't think wis possible.

Best Swordfencers: the back o' the bus.

Best Singers: the back o' the bus.

The Longest Sleeper: you know who you are.

The Quickest Magooed: same person that wis the longest sleeper.

The Strangest Fetish: the same person that wis the longest sleeper and the quickest Magooed . . . was into sniffing the tarmac at every car park we stopped at on the way down.

All in all . . . another cracking trip wi' a brilliant bunch of guys and gals.

And Dianne's report (posted by Dianne on 5:58 pm on 20 May 2002):

My fave moments from Wales:

Making light-sabres for the children on the bus. Beating the blokes at killer darts – even though you play crappy rules, I still kicked yer erses! Wearing the MASSIVE shoes at the game and running around like a fool (I know, nothing new!) Winning 2–0 – always nice.

The (one song) Welsh. What a great bunch of people. My dad standing in between the home and away management with the megaphone, singing 'Flower of Scotland' . . . The team couldn't sing it for laughing. Tommy's Tantric Tartan Army . . . You really had to be there, sooo funny (camera 1 camera 2) Strangest Fetish must go to Sammy – sniffing Julie Fleeting's shin guard . . . minger.

And here's some of Di's songbook, starting with a wee couplet from Sonny in praise of the Welsh people's least favourite person:

> *Here's to you, Anne Robinson,*
> *Scotland loves you more than you will know . . .*

Bridie Boy supplied the following:

> *We're on the march wi' Vera's Army*
> *We're all going to Merthyr Tyd*
> *And the Taffs'll all get shocks*
> *When we flash Fiona's bollocks*
> *'Cause the Scots girls are the greatest of them all.*

It should be pointed out that Fiona is a pheasant. A stuffed pheasant, in case the fur-and-feather huggers are worried. She goes to all the games, male and female, so if anyone asks, we can always say that we got a burd at every game.

denhaagdavid (You'll never guess where he stays) fancies himself, with some justification, as the official TAMB poet. He couldn't make the game, but sent this for the songsheet:

> *I awoke in the night with a fever,*
> *The sky was the darkest blue,*
> *And I heard a woman's voice calling,*
> *'The women are needing you!'*
> *Next thing I know I'm in Wales,*
> *Watching women playing football . . . again,*
> *And I see the manager calling me*
> *'Come on, get stripped, you're on!'*
> *I have a dream, a dream come true,*
> *That Scotland's ladies,*
> *(That Scotland's ladies)*
> *I'll be showering with you.*

In your dreams indeed, David. David speaks for many, sexist pig that he is. He is, however, a funny sexist pig. So that's OK then. Here's Fringo's dream. The tune might have something to do with the Proclaimers.

> *When we kilt up, yeah we know you're gonna see*
> *Gonna see us wear our kilts with pride for you*

When we follow, yeah we know we're gonna be
We're gonna be the ones who always follow you

If we get drunk, yes we know we're gonna be
We're gonna be the ones who are gonna get Magooed
And if we haver, yes we know we're gonna be
We're gonna be the ones who are havering for you

Chorus
But we would walk 500 miles
And we would walk 500 more
Just to be the ones who walked 1000 miles
To see Bonnie Scotland score

When we're singing, yes we know we're gonna be
We're gonna be the ones who are singing just for you
When we're cheering, yes we know we're gonna cheer
We're gonna cheer all night and day for you.

When you're lonely, yes we know we're gonna be
We're gonna be there to make you strong and true
When we're dreaming, yes we know we're gonna dream
Dream about the girls in Scotland's blue

Chorus

To digress briefly. At the last away Iceland game there was a new twist on the chorus of '500 Miles'. Instead of:

'*BAAARUMMBA, BAAARRUMMBA,*
BARUMDIDDLEUMDIDDLE DA DA DA . . .'

in the middle, we sang:

'GERRIT UP YEEZ, GERRIT UP YEEZ,
BARUMDIDDLEUMDIDDLE DA DA DA . . .'

Fringo claims to be a physio in disguise. Would I be alone in suspecting an ulterior motive? Or maybe it is an anterior motive. He does seem to be interested in women's fronts.

Here's Bridie Boy again with his own version of:

TAFFY WHAUR'S YER BOOZERS?

We came on a bus on a long, long drive
We're here to see Scotland win Group Five
We wear the kilts and we jump and jive
Taffy whaur's yer boozers?

Some of us couldny come this far
So we brought along their avatar
And we take them along to see all the bars
Oh, Taffy whaur's yer boozers?

Well there's some of us that don't exist
But we're all here to drink and to get pissed
We'll see Scotland, they won't be missed
(Elvis-style) Taffy a-where's ya boozers?

methilstevie seems to be a fan of the Beach Boys. He calls this:

AH WISH THEY ALL COULD BE CALEDONIAN GURLZZZZZ

Well, East Fife's girls are hip, I really dig those kilts
they wear
And the Glasgow girls, with the way they drink,
They knock me out when I'm down there
Dundee's dealer's daughters really make me feel alright
And the Dingwall girls, with the way they kiss,
They keep their boyfriends warm at night

And every establishment in Wales that we entered was blessed with:

We're the famous Tartan Army and we're here
to get Magooed
Get Magooed! Get Magooed!
We're the famous Tartan Army and we're here to get
Magooed

Funnily enough, they knew what we meant. Fringo, though he wasn't there, can have the final word, as he tailors this one for wherever we go:

Chorus
From the valleys high to the valleys low
On Blackie's bus in our kilts we'll go
And all we ever want to know is
Taffy whaur's yer boozers?

Well there's some of us frae Inverurie
Some called Ian, Dianne and Ruary
Some are sheep, real, virtual and furry
Taffy whaur's yer boozers?

Chorus

We'll drink the beer, wine, any booze
Win or draw, but we'll never lose
We're here to cheer and get Magooed
Taffy whaur's yer boozers?

Chorus

We've been to Livvy in April and May
We're going to Merthyr this Saturday
To cheer for Scotland on the day
Taffy whaur's yer boozers?

Chorus

The bus is booked and we're raring to go
We've got the fridge and the video
And a wee kerry-oot as well . . . for the road
Taffy whaur's yer boozers?

Chorus

And the obsession with the women grows. We are now talking travelling to away games on a continuing basis, we are talking Prague and Kiev. We are talking Lionheart travelling to and then across Portugal on his own to see them play, we are talking America and the world waking up to the fact that Julie Fleeting is one of the best strikers on the planet and that we have other people who can play a bit.

And we are also now talking Bridie Boy, aka Allan Whyte, writing the following for the object of his affections:

GEMMA FAY
Tune: 'Yesterday'

Gemma Fay, you play for Scotland and you're top tot-tay,
And if you fancy me well that's okay,
Oh, I believe in Gemma Fay.

Suddenly, you had a restraining order put on me,
I know you're kidding 'cause once you smiled at me
You're such a joker, Gemma Fay

Why she plays in goals I don't know, she wouldn't say
I shout 'SAVE THE BALL' how we all love Gemma
Fay-ay-ay-ay-ay, Gemma Fay . . .

. . . and so on until your throat bursts. Allan suggests that this could be the new 'Doh-a-Deer'. God help us one and all, but we did sing it at the game at which Allan produced his songsheet and it is beginning to catch on.

To confuse the police and the civil authorities, he also wrote a song about each of the squad, aided and abetted by other fanatics. Here are some more:

JULIE SMITH
Tune: 'Let Me Entertain You' Robbie Williams

The men are gone and heaven's here
There nothing left for us to fear
Shake your ass come over here
Now scream

We support the wimmin's team
'Cause they're the best we've ever seen
Hold the ball but keep it clean
My dear

So come on pass to-ooo-ooo Julie Smi-ith
Pass to-ooo-ooo Julie Smi-ith

MEGAN SNEDDON
Tune: 'White Wedding' Billy Idol

Hey little sister what have you done
Hey little sister who's the only one

Hey little sister who's your superman
Hey little sister who's the one you want
Hey little sister shotgun

It's a nice day to start again
It's a nice day for a Megan Sneddon
It's a nice day to start again

PAULINE HAMILL
Tune: 'Cheeky Girls'

Oooh ah smiler girl
Oooh ah smiler girl
Ooooooooooooohhhhhhhh
She is the smiler girl,
She is the smiler girl,
We are the Tartan boys,
We are the Tartan boys,
She is the smiler girl,
She is the smiler girl,
We are the Tartan boys,
We are the Tartan boys, etc.

JULIE FERGUSON
Tune: 'Supercalifra....'

Julie Ferguson can mix it with the best in Europe
She can play most any day
To bring us back to the top
If we cheer her loud enough
She'll score the goals that we need
Julie Ferguson can mix it with the best in Europe

JULIE FLEETING
Tune: 'You've Lost That Lovin' Feeling'

We've got that Julie Fleeting,
Oh-o-that Julie Fleeting,
We've got that Julie Fleeting
And she score scores scores, whoa-oh-o
Duh-rum, duh-rum, duh-rum-dum

Julie, Julie I'll get down on my knees for you,
If you would only score goals, like you norm'ly
do-oo-oo-oo-oo-oo-oo-ooo-oo
You lay the ball off and pass it over to the left,
It then gets crossed in, you jump and head into the net.
Baby, baby, baby, baby, etc.

CLAIRE JOHNSTONE
Tune: 'I'm sorry Miss Jackson' Outkast

I'm sorry Claire Johnstone, oooh
I am for real
Never meant to buy a greasy pie,
I apologise a trillion times
etc.

SUZANNE ROBERTSON
Tune: 'Mrs Robinson'

So here's to you Suzy Robertson
The Tartan Army loves you, do you know (woh-oh-oh)
Now hold the ball Suzy Robertson,
Thread it through for us to score a goal (go-o-o-al)

MICHELLE BARR
Tune: 'I Like Driving in my Car' Madness

We support you Michelle Barr
You play for Scotland you're a star,
We drive up to Almondvale
And thank God that you're not male

No there is no-one we fear
Because we are in the top tier,
They'll hear us all from near and far,
'WE ALL LOVE YOU MICHELLE BARR'

SHELLEY KERR
Tune: 'You're Just Too Good To Be True'
Andy Williams

We love you Shelley,
And if it's quite alright,
We love you Shelley,
Always put up a fight,
We love you Shelley,
You're loved by Tartan Army,

Oh, Auntie Shelley,
Please stop them getting through,
Oh, Auntie Shelley,
We'll always follow you,

Oh, Auntie Shelley Tartan
Army loves you,
You're just to good to be true!

STACEY COOK
Tune: 'Always Look on . . .' Monty Python

Some things in life are bad,
They can really make you mad,
Men's football just makes you swear and curse,
When your pie is full of gristle
Don't grumble, give a whistle (wolf whistle)
We've got the best defender over there, aaaannnnddd,

Stacey Cook is the best in the land,
(Whistle) etc.

NICKY GRANT
Tune: 'What's New Pussycat?' Tom Jones

What's new Nicky Grant whoa-whoa-whoa-oh,
What's new Nicky Grant whoa-whoa-whoa-oh-oh,
Nicky Grant, Nicky Grant I love you, yes I do,
You and your Nicky Grant boots whoa-whoa-oh
You and your Nicky Grant eyes whoa-whoa-oh
You and your Nicky Grant hair whoa-whoa-oh etc.

SUZANNE GRANT
Tune: 'Super Gran'

*Stand back Engerlund, Iceland, Netherlands, Belgium and
Ireland too
Don't want to cause a ruckus with BA Barracus, 'cause
we've got a match for you,
She makes the men look like a bunch of fairies,
got more bottle than Christian Dailly
Hang about, look out for Suzanne Grant*

AMANDA BURNS
Tune: 'Ring of Fire' Johnny Cash

*A-man-da Burns Burns Burns
She's on fi-re
She's on fire*

JULIA RALPH
Tune: Campbelltown Loch

*Julia Ralph, I wish you were frisky
Julia Ralph, och aye
Julia Ralph, I wish you were frisky
I'm going for a pie*

Oh Julia Ralph is a wonderful girl
And she spends every night at the gym
How nice it would be
If she came on to me
Oh, I'd even buy her a gin

JOANNE LOVE
Tune: 'Yellow' by Coldplay

Look at Joanne,
Look how she plays for you,
And holds the ball up too,
Oh we call her J-Lo.

We came along,
And wrote a song for you,
And all the things you do,
And we love you J-Lo.

You skii-iiiin – defenders one by one
Pass-iiing – them all just for fun
You know
You know we love J-Lo
You know we love J-Lo

MHAIRI GILMOUR
Tune: 'Donald Whaur's Yer Troosers'

Let's play football, here we go,
Scotland's gonna score a goal,
The Tartan Army roar and roar,
all for Mhairi Gilmour.

Allan didn't quite manage a song for everyone. Here's what he said on the songsheet:

'Apologies for not having songs for Mellissa Donachie and Linda Brown as we didn't have time to make them up. We spent ages trying to think of one for Mellissa and got nowhere and didn't have time to re-word 'Bad, Bad Leroy Brown' for Linda!!!! COME ON THE GIRLS!!'

Damn' slacker. He also wishes to implicate the following accomplices: Sacks (Steven Ricketts, let the record stand, m'lud) wrote the Amanda Burns one and Dianne (Small, ditto, m'lud) wrote the Mhairi Gilmour one.

A new tradition has grown up at Almondvale, where the women play their home games, of singing the team onto the park. It starts, to the tune of 'He's Got the Whole World in His Hands' . . .

We've got Vera Pauw, manager

And continues:

We've got Gemma Fay, number one . . . and so on.

This is greatly aided by the fact that teamsheets are distributed throughout the crowd, an initiative of which Lisa Brown of the SWFA should be proud.

And of course a special one for the manager, Vera Pauw.

VERA PAUW
Tune: 'Que Sera, Sera'

Hey Vera, Vera
Please give us a wave Vera
We'll buy you a beer Vera
Hey Vera, Vera.

When we went to Lithuania in 2003 for the Euro qualifier we found out what the word 'Baltic' really meant. We were standing there, some guys just in tops, and it was twelve degrees below. I was wearing every stitch of clothing that I could find, and bitterly regretting not putting on the dirty clothes as well, as the guy beside me happily pointed out he had done.

Hailstones are normally round and while they sometimes sting you, they don't draw blood. What we got there were frozen, sharp-edged snowflakes. They actually cut your face. And what were we singing?

Here for the sun tan.
We're only here for the sun tan.
Here for the su-u-un tan.
We're only here for the sun tan.

And at the friendly in Portugal, standing in the biggest downpour I have ever seen, umbrellas abandoned as a joke, drenched to the skin, frozen to the bone, pitch flooded and making a farce of the game, what are we singing?

Score at the deep end
Youse only score at the deep end

In Lithuania I was part of a delegation from the Tartan Army Sunshine Appeal, our charity, which gives gifts and money to people less fortunate than us in the countries that we visit. We visited an orphanage in Vilnius, taking them video recorders, tellies, laptops, and a whole lot of other stuff, including backpacks that we had filled with toys and other things for the kids, mostly brought over by footsoldiers on their backs. We also filled backpacks for a home for kids in a place called Zagare, on the border with Latvia, and I raised a few bob for them by stopping drinking for a week. Here's what the headmistress sent us:

TO ALL THE TARTAN ARMY MEMBERS WHO
HELPED WITH THE SUNSHINE APPEAL
DONATION TO LITHUANIA LINK IN ZAGARE
Thank you for the joyful and happy moments which you gave us with your sincere gifts. Your support gave us a chance to spend our leisure more meaningful and variously. We felt your hearts' warmness and love for other people.

Thank you, dear people.

On behalf of all the children and teachers in the boarding school in Zagare.

Headmistress, Angele Kareckiene

I don't want to bang on too much about this, but it is one of the more worthwhile things that I've done, and I'd like to thank all of the people who worked so hard and all the people who donated. You know who you are. Diamonds every one of you. It was an abiding and deep pleasure to be part of it. Standing in that orphanage with my eyes filled with tears, I felt as proud to be Scottish and a footsoldier in the Tartan Army as I have ever felt.

I have since been to Zagare and stayed in the Home. They have nothing. They can use virtually anything. Money is best, though, and you can send it to Lithuania

Link, who are at: Beech House, Curthwaite, Wigton, Cumbria, CA7 8BG. Tel/fax: (+44) (0)1228 710 347. By email: info@lithuanialink.org.

Or you can give it to me and I'll see that it gets there. I'm at the games, usually wearing a TAMB T-shirt with my name on it, and in the pub before and after, enjoying a small dry sherry and the company of my comrades-in-arms. Thanks.

And finally, according to the *Encyclopedia Brittanica*, the second most-sung song in the world. Happy Birthday' is the most sung. This is Rabbie's and Scotland's gift to drunks and nostalgia junkies everywhere. Could everyone learn the words, please, because, according to the *Encyclopedia Blackiea*, it is also the least known, lyrics-wise. Where does 'We'll meet again some other nicht' and 'the days of' nonsense that I keep hearing come from? It is a truly great tune and the sentiment is universal. Bit of respect up the back there for the National Bard, please.

David Taylor and I agree that there is a case for this becoming our national song. I'm doing my best, David. I think that verses one and four, with choruses, should be the ones, with the team and the fans joining hands on: *'And there's a hand my trusty fiere,'* and giving it laldy in traditional style.

AULD LANG SYNE

<u>Words adapted from a traditional song
by Rabbie Burns (1759-96)</u>

Should auld acquaintance be forgot,
And never brought to mind?
Should auld acquaintance be forgot,
And auld lang syne?

Chorus
For auld lang syne, my dear,
For auld lang syne,
We'll tak a cup of kindness yet,
For auld lang syne!

Chorus

We twa hae run about the braes,
And pou'd the gowans fine,
But we've wander'd monie a weary fit,
Sin auld lang syne.

Chorus

We twa hae paidl'd in the burn,
Frae morning sun till dine,
But seas between us braid hae roar'd,
Sin auld lang syne.

Chorus

And there's a hand my trusty fiere,
And gie's a hand o thine,
And we'll tak a right guid willie waught,
For auld lang syne.

Chorus

And surely ye'll be your pint-stowp,
And surely I'll be mine,
And we'll tak a cup o kindness yet,
For auld lang syne!